Mary Norwak was born in London and now
lives in Norfolk. She has been a journalist for
over twenty years, contributing regularly to
the food columns in the National Press and to
other magazines. She is at present editor of a
consumer magazine on home freezing. Her
publications include *The Pie Book*, *Fridge
and Freezer Cookbook*, *The Fruit Book* and
The Complete Book of Barbecues.

*Also by Mary Norwak and available
from Sphere Books*

DEEP FREEZING
A–Z OF HOME FREEZING
DEEP FREEZING MENUS & RECIPES
HOME FREEZING: A BEGINNERS GUIDE
GROWING, FREEZING & COOKING (with Keith Mossman)
MIXER & BLENDER COOKBOOK

A Calendar of
Home Freezing

MARY NORWAK

SPHERE BOOKS LIMITED
30/32 Gray's Inn Road, London WC1X 8JL

First published in Great Britain by Sphere Books Ltd 1972
Reprinted 1974
Copyright © Mary Norwak 1972
Revised edition published 1976

Set in Monotype Plantin

Printed in Great Britain by
Hazell Watson & Viney Ltd
Aylesbury, Bucks

CONTENTS

5

INTRODUCTION

This Calendar is designed for all those busy women to whom the food freezer is now an essential piece of equipment. Keen gardeners, farmers or sportsmen will not need to be reminded of the seasonal cycles of fruit and vegetables, meat, poultry, game and fish; but their wives may be glad to have their memories jogged so that they can be prepared for the sometimes overwhelming sacks, bags and boxes of raw materials. Included in the Calendar are instructions for preparing and freezing glut quantities of fruit and vegetables in a variety of ways, so that less space is taken up in the freezer, and monotony is avoided in meals.

In the summer months, most time is spent in freezing raw materials, but cooked dishes must not be forgotten for holiday times. In the winter, more space can be given to cooked dishes, and in particular to foods prepared for Christmas and parties. The Calendar reminds housewives of the ways to use seasonal foods, of the bargains to be found in the shops, of the bulk items to stock up on for school holidays, and of prepare-ahead dishes for family meals and entertaining.

Obviously, many foods have quite a long season, but each item has only been included in the month in which it is most likely to be in good supply and of high quality at a low price.

ALL THE YEAR ROUND

Many raw materials can now be bought all through the year, and there is little point in freezing them unless there is plenty of space available. If quality is high and prices are really low, they can be frozen if the family likes them. Instructions for freezing are given in the months when the best supplies are likely to be available.

FRUIT
Melons, oranges, pineapples.

VEGETABLES
Aubergines, broccoli, cabbage, courgettes, mushrooms, peppers, spinach, tomatoes.

FISH (*quality drops when spawning*)
Cod, halibut, herrings, plaice, shrimps, sole, trout, turbot.

POULTRY AND GAME
Capons, chicken, duck, pigeon, rabbit, turkey.

MEAT
Beef, pork.

JANUARY

In the early part of the month, it is still necessary to cook and freeze party dishes. Later in the month, it is a good time to stock up on game which is in good supply, but the season is drawing to a close. Citrus fruit and marmalade oranges are worth preserving, and there are post-Christmas bargains of dried fruit in the shops, worth saving in the freezer.

FOOD IN SEASON

Vegetables Brussels sprouts, cabbage, carrots, cauliflower, celery, chicory, leeks, parsnips, turnips.
Fruit Cooking apples, cranberries, grapefruit, lemons, oranges, Seville oranges for marmalade, early rhubarb.
Fish Cod, haddock, mackerel, mussels, oysters, scallops, sole, sprats, turbot, whiting.
Meat, Poultry and Game Goose, turkey, hare, partridge, pheasant, pigeon, plover, snipe, wild duck, woodcock.

WHAT TO BUY FROM THE SHOPS
Dates, figs, glacé fruit.

BULK BUYING CHECKLIST
New Zealand lamb.

NOW IS THE TIME TO FREEZE:

Chicory, cranberries, grapefruit, lemons, oranges, Seville oranges, dried fruit, glacé fruit

CHICORY

Chicory cannot be used as a salad vegetable after freezing. It is worth freezing to serve as a vegetable or part of a composite dish. Use compact heads with yellow tips, trim stalks and remove any bruised outside leaves. Blanch for 2 minutes, adding 2 tbsp lemon juice to blanching water to prevent browning. Chicory absorbs a lot of water and must be well drained. Pack in waxed boxes or plastic containers. *To serve*: Cook in stock, or braise with butter as for the fresh vegetable. *Storage time:* 6 months.

CRANBERRIES

Cranberries should be firm, well-coloured and glossy, without mealiness. Fruit should be carefully sorted, omitting any shrivelled or soft berries, washed in cold water and drained. As they will most likely be converted into sauce at a later date, they are best packed dry and unsweetened in bags or containers. If purée is preferred, cook the berries gently in very little water until the skins pop; put through a sieve and add sugar to taste (about 8 oz. sugar to each pint of purée). Pack into containers, allowing $\frac{1}{2}$ in. headspace. *To serve:* Thaw at room temperature for $3\frac{1}{2}$ hours. *Storage time:* 1 year.

GRAPEFRUIT

Peel the fruit, removing all pith, and cut segments away from pith. Pack dry with sugar (8 oz. sugar to 2 breakfast cups of segments) in cartons, or pack in 50% syrup (16 oz. sugar to 1 pint water). *To serve:* Thaw at room temperature for 2½ hours. *Storage time:* 1 year.

LEMONS

Lemon slices can be stored in the freezer, and also lemon juice and lemon peel.

Lemon slices or wedges can be frozen peeled or unpeeled to be used as a garnish, or in drinks. If unpeeled, they can be frozen dry in bags, and used as soon as thawed. If peeled, freeze in 20% syrup (4 oz. sugar to 1 pint water). *To serve:* Thaw at room temperature for 1 hour. *Storage time:* 1 year.

Lemon juice is most easily frozen in ice-cube trays, and each cube then wrapped in foil and packaged in quantity in polythene, to be used for drinks or for cooking. *Storage time:* 1 year.

Lemon peel can be grated finely and packed in small waxed or rigid plastic containers. It should be thawed in container at room temperature to use for cakes and puddings. *Storage time:* 1 year.

ORANGES

Sweet oranges can be frozen in sections, but pack better if frozen in slices. Peel fruit and remove all pith, and cut flesh in ¼-in. slices, then proceed by one of these methods:

(*a*) Use a dry sugar pack, allowing 8 oz. sugar to 3 breakfast cups of orange pieces, and pack in containers or polythene bags.

(b) Use 30% syrup (7 oz. sugar to 1 pint water) and pack oranges in waxed or rigid plastic containers, covering with Cellophane and leaving $\frac{1}{2}$ in. headspace

(c) Pack slices in slightly sweetened fresh orange juice in cartons.

It is worth noting that navel oranges develop a bitter flavour when frozen. *To serve:* Thaw $2\frac{1}{2}$ hours at room temperature. *Storage time:* 1 year.

Orange peel can be grated and frozen in small waxed or plastic containers to use for flavouring cakes, puddings and preserves.

Storage time: 2 months.

SEVILLE ORANGES

Bitter oranges for marmalade may be frozen whole in their skins in polythene bags, to use later for marmalade. Pack in half-dozens or dozens according to recipe quantities likely to be used.

DRIED FRUIT

Dates and *dried figs* freeze very well. If dates are frozen in the boxes they are packed in they tend to dry out and acquire off-flavours. When good quality fruit is available, remove stones and freeze fruit in polythene bags or in waxed cartons. Block dates may be wrapped in foil or put into polythene bags (to avoid stickiness, they may be left in their original wrappings before being put into freezer packaging). Frozen dates may be eaten raw, or used for cakes and puddings. *Dried dessert figs* may be wrapped in foil or polythene bags, and are useful in the freezer since they have only a short season. *Storage time:* 1 year.

GLACÉ FRUIT

Keep glacé fruit in its original box and over-wrap with a polythene bag. Separate pieces of fruit can be wrapped in foil and packaged in quantities in polythene. *To serve:* Thaw in wrappings at room temperature for 3 hours before using. *Storage time:* 1 year.

WHEN THERE'S A GLUT, FREEZE:

Citrus Fruit Juice

CITRUS FRUIT JUICE

Use oranges, grapefruit, lemons or limes, making sure fruit is of good quality, heavy in the hand for its size. Chill unpeeled fruit in ice water or in the refrigerator until ready to extract juice. Squeeze juice and strain. Pack in waxed or rigid plastic containers, leaving $\frac{1}{2}$ in. headspace. Lemon and lime juice may be frozen in ice-cube trays, each cube being wrapped in foil when frozen. *To serve:* Thaw at room temperature for 1 hour and sweeten to taste. Small cubes of lemon or lime juice are very useful for individual drinks. *Storage time:* 1 year.

PREPARE-AHEAD DISHES

SCOTCH BROTH

1 lb lean neck of mutton	1 onion
4 pints water	1 carrot
1 leek	1 turnip
2 sticks celery	Sprig of parsley
	Salt and pepper

Cut meat into small squares and simmer in water for 1 hour. Add vegetables cut in dice, parsley and seasoning, and continue cooking gently for 1½ hours. Cool and remove fat, and take out parsley.

Pack into containers, leaving headspace.

To serve: Reheat gently in saucepan and add 2 tbsp barley, simmering until barley is tender.

Storage time: 2 months.

COCK-A-LEEKIE

1 boiling chicken	1 small tsp black pepper
1 lb shin beef	2 level tsp salt
6 leeks	
4 oz. prunes	

Wipe the chicken inside and out and put into a large saucepan. Cut meat into small pieces. Clean and slice leeks thinly, using some of the green parts. Add salt and pepper and cover with cold water. Bring to simmering point and cook gently for 4 hours. Add the prunes and simmer 45 minutes. Take out the chicken and cut flesh into neat small pieces, return to saucepan and reheat.

Pack into containers, leaving headspace.

To serve: Reheat gently, adjusting seasoning.

Storage time: 2 months.

COD'S ROE PÂTÉ

12 oz. smoked cod's roe
1 gill double cream
1 crushed garlic clove
Juice of ½ lemon
1 dsp olive oil
Black pepper

Scrape roe into a bowl and mix to a smooth paste with cream, garlic, lemon, oil and pepper.

Pack into small containers with lids.

To serve: Thaw in refrigerator for 3 hours, stirring occasionally to blend ingredients.

Storage time: 1 month.

HARE PÂTÉ

1½ lb uncooked hare
¼ lb fat bacon
3 tbsp brandy
¾ lb minced pork and veal
Salt, pepper and nutmeg
1 egg

A mixture of game and rabbit can also be used for this recipe. Cut the hare into small pieces and the bacon into dice and mix together in a dish with brandy. Leave for 1 hour, then put through mincer with pork and veal. Season, add egg and mix well. Press mixture into a buttered container, cover with greased paper and lid and put dish in a baking tin of water. Bake at 400°F (Gas Mark 6) for 1 hour. Leave under weights until cold.

Pack by covering container with foil lid and sealing with freezer tape, or by repacking in heavy-duty foil. This is only advisable if a large amount of pâté is to be eaten at once. Otherwise repack mixture into small containers and cover before freezing (if the pâté is cooked in small containers, it will be dry).

To serve: Thaw small containers at room temperature for 1 hour. Thaw large pâté in wrappings in refrigerator for 6 hours, or at room temperature for 3 hours. Use immediately after thawing.

Storage time: 1 month.

GAME PIE

1½ lb uncooked hare	Pepper and salt
½ lb uncooked pheasant or rabbit	4 oz. mushrooms
	1 pint brown gravy
¼ lb calves' or lambs' liver	1 bay leaf
	12 oz. short pastry
2 oz. butter or dripping	

Cut flesh away from bones of hare, pheasant or rabbit, and cut in neat pieces. Cut liver in small pieces. Season well and brown lightly in a pan. Turn into a pie dish with mushrooms, gravy and bay leaf. Cover with pastry and bake at 350°F (Gas Mark 4) for 1½ hours. Use a pie dish which can be put in the freezer, or a foil dish. Cool pie completely before freezing.

Pack by covering dish with heavy-duty foil.

To serve: Thaw at room temperature for 4 hours to eat cold, or heat at 400°F (Gas Mark 6) for 40 minutes to eat hot.

Storage time: 2 months.

OXTAIL STEW

1 oxtail	4 medium carrots
1 oz. dripping	2 cloves
1 oz. plain flour	Salt and pepper
1 medium onion	

Wipe oxtail and cut into joints. Dust lightly

with flour, and fry the joints in dripping until light brown. Work in any remaining flour and add 1½ pints water. Bring to the boil, then add sliced onion and cloves, and season to taste. Simmer for 2 hours. Add sliced carrots and continue cooking for 10 minutes. Cool completely and take off fat, and remove cloves.

Pack into containers, leaving headspace.

To serve: Reheat gently, adjusting seasoning to taste, and add 2 tbsp sherry.

Storage time: 2 months.

POT ROAST CHICKEN

3-lb chicken	2 medium carrots
1½ oz. butter	1 small turnip
2 sticks celery	½ pint stock
6 small onions	Salt and pepper

Wipe chicken inside and out. Melt butter and brown chicken lightly on all sides. Add sliced vegetables, stock, and salt and pepper. Cover and simmer for 1½ hours, basting sometimes with stock. This dish may be cooked on top of the stove, or in an oven set at 375°F (Gas Mark 5). Cool completely and take off fat.

Pack in container, leaving headspace.

To serve: Return to casserole and heat at 350°F (Gas Mark 4) for 45 minutes. Garnish with chopped parsley before serving.

Storage time: 2 months.

BAKED STUFFED LIVER

1½ lb liver	½ tsp salt
1 oz. flour	¼ tsp pepper
6 oz. bacon	1 small onion
2 tbsp breadcrumbs	¼ tsp grated lemon
1 tsp chopped	rind
parsley	½ pint stock

Toss liver in flour and put into a shallow tin or oven dish. Mix together breadcrumbs, parsley, salt and pepper, finely chopped onion and lemon rind, and moisten with a little stock. Spread over liver and top each slice with a rasher of bacon. Pour on stock and bake at 375°F (Gas Mark 5) for 35 minutes. Cool completely.

Pack in container, or cover cooking dish with heavy-duty foil lid.

To serve: Reheat at 350°F (Gas Mark 4) for 30 minutes.

Storage time: 1 month.

PRETORIA PUDDING

8 oz. fresh white	4 oz. moist brown
breadcrumbs	sugar
8 oz. peeled apples	3 eggs
4 oz. currants	1 tsp grated nutmeg

Put the apples through the mincer, and mix with crumbs and currants. Stir in the sugar, beaten eggs and nutmeg. Pour into a foil pudding basin and steam for 2 hours. Cool completely.

Pack by covering with a foil lid.

To serve: Steam for 1 hour directly from the freezer, and serve with syrup.

Storage time: 2 months.

RHUBARB BROWN BETTY

4 oz. fresh white	1 lb early rhubarb
breadcrumbs	3 tbsp water
2 oz. butter	2 tbsp golden syrup
2 oz. sugar	

Rub the butter into the breadcrumbs and add the sugar. Put a layer of this mixture into a dish which will go in the freezer (e.g. oven-glass or foil). Cut rhubarb into neat pieces and put a layer on the crumbs. Continue in crumb and rhubarb layers, finishing with crumbs. Dissolve the syrup in the water and pour over the mixture. Bake at 350°F (Gas Mark 4) for 40 minutes. Cool completely.

Pack by covering dish with heavy-duty foil lid.

To serve: Heat at 350°F (Gas Mark 4) for 45 minutes, and serve with cream or custard.

Storage time: 2 months.

BAKED STUFFED APPLES

6 cooking apples	6 tsp soft brown
3 tbsp golden syrup	sugar
6 dates	1 oz. butter
Grated rind of 1	4 tbsp water
orange	

Wipe and core apples and cut round skin of each round the centre. Put into a buttered oven dish. In the middle of each put a little syrup, a date, a pinch of orange rind, a tsp of sugar and a knob of butter. Put water in dish, and bake at 350°F (Gas Mark 4) for 45 minutes. Cool completely.

Pack in a foil dish, separating apples with Cellophane or foil. Apples may be packed individually in cartons.

To serve: Thaw at room temperature for 1 hour to eat cold with cream. Apples may be reheated in a moderate oven, and served hot with cream.

Storage time: 2 months.

STEAMED GOLDEN SPONGE

5 oz. self-raising flour	3 oz. caster sugar
Pinch of salt	2 eggs
3 oz. butter or margarine	1 dsp milk
	Grated rind of $\frac{1}{2}$ orange or lemon

Mix flour and salt. Beat fat until soft, add sugar and beat until light and fluffy. Work in eggs one at a time, with a little flour. Beat in milk, rind and a little flour, then stir in remaining flour.

Pack in foil basin, leaving 1 in. headspace, and cover with foil.

To serve: Steam for 2 hours directly from the freezer, and serve with jam, syrup or fruit sauce.

Storage time: 2 months.

CALIFORNIA CAKE

5 eggs	2 tsp baking
7 oz. caster sugar	powder
8 oz. plain flour	1 tsp lemon juice
Pinch of salt	4 fl. oz. orange juice

Separate eggs, and beat the yolks until foamy. Add half the sugar and continue to beat until the sugar has dissolved. Sift flour, salt and baking powder and add alternately with the fruit juices. Whip egg whites until stiff, fold in remaining sugar, and fold into cake mixture. Put into 8-in. cake tin, and bake at 350°F for 1 hour. Cool completely.

Pack in polythene bag or in heavy-duty foil.

To serve: Thaw at room temperature for 3 hours, and dust with icing sugar.

Storage time: 2 months.

BLACKMORE VALE HUNT CAKE

4 oz. butter	1 tsp bicarbonate
4 oz. caster sugar	of soda
12 oz. plain flour	1 dsp golden syrup
3 fl. oz. milk	12 oz. stoned raisins
	3 oz. candied peel

Beat butter and sugar until soft and fluffy. Warm milk until tepid and stir in syrup and bicarbonate of soda. Add flour gradually to the butter mixture alternately with the flour. Beat well and add raisins and peel. Pour into 7-in. cake tin and bake at 350°F (Gas Mark 4) for 1 hour 45 minutes. Cool completely on rack.

Pack in polythene bag or in heavy-duty foil.

To serve: Thaw at room temperature for 3 hours.

Storage time: 2 months.

CHERRY ALMOND CAKE

7 oz. self-raising flour
Pinch of salt
4 oz. butter or
    margarine
4 oz. caster sugar
3 eggs
1 oz. ground almonds
6 oz. glacé cherries

Wash and dry cherries. Mix flour and salt. Cut up cherries in 4 pieces, and toss in a little of the flour. Cream butter or margarine until soft, and add sugar, beating until light and fluffy. Beat in eggs one at a time with a little of the flour. Stir in almonds, cherries and remaining flour. Put into greased and lined 6-in. tin. Bake at 350°F (Gas Mark 4) for 1 hour 20 minutes. Cool completely.

Pack in polythene bag or in heavy-duty foil.

To serve: Thaw at room temperature for 3 hours.

Storage time: 2 months.

FEBRUARY

There is not much fresh food worth preserving this month, since many raw materials are coming to the end of their season. This makes a good month for stocking up with casseroles, puddings and cakes, and of course pancakes for Shrove Tuesday. There is still time to freeze citrus fruit, and to freeze early rhubarb in the form of pies and compôtes. This is also a good time for imported lamb.

FOOD IN SEASON

Vegetables Brussels sprouts, cabbage, cauliflower, celery, chicory, leeks, parsnips.
Fruit Cooking apples, grapefruit, Seville oranges for marmalade, early rhubarb.
Meat, Poultry and Game Hare.

BULK BUYING CHECKLIST
New Zealand lamb.

NOW IS THE TIME TO FREEZE:

Leeks, early rhubarb

LEEKS

Wash leeks very thoroughly and cut in rings. Blanch for 1 minute and pack in boxes or bags. *To serve:* Add to soups and stews, or cook 5 minutes in boiling water and serve with white sauce as a vegetable. *Storage time:* 2 months.

RHUBARB

Rhubarb should be frozen while it is young and pink. The sticks may be most easily frozen unsweetened to use in pies or fools later. Wash the sticks in cold running water, trim to desired length and pack in cartons, foil or polythene bags. To make packing easier, stalks may be blanched for 1 minute, making them slightly limp, and the colour and flavour will be better preserved by this method. Rhubarb can also be cut into shorter lengths and packed in 40% syrup (11 oz. sugar to 1 pint water) in cartons. Stewed rhubarb can be sieved and sweetened and frozen as purée, but it is a pity to waste the first early rhubarb in this way. *To serve:* Thaw at room temperature for 3½ hours. *Storage time:* 1 year.

PREPARE-AHEAD DISHES

PIGEON PÂTÉ

3 pigeons	Salt and pepper
8 fl. oz. red wine	4 onions
4 fl. oz. vinegar	8 oz. sausage meat
1 bay leaf	1 slice of bread
1 small tsp thyme	A little milk
Grating of nutmeg	

Joint the pigeons. Mix together wine, vinegar, bay leaf, thyme, nutmeg, salt and pepper and finely chopped onions, and pour this over the birds. Leave to soak in cool place for 3 days. Remove flesh from the birds, and mince twice. Mix with sausage meat. Remove crusts from the bread, and soak in enough milk to moisten the bread. Beat this into the meat mixture. Press mixture into a terrine, loaf tin, or oven dish and cover with a lid or foil. Stand dish in a tin of water, and cook at 350°F (Gas Mark 4) for 1½ hours. Cool completely under weights. Remove from baking dish.

Pack in heavy-duty foil.

To serve: Thaw at room temperature for 3 hours.

Storage time: 2 months.

HARE MOULD

½ lb jugged hare	2 tbsp redcurrant
Forcemeat balls	jelly
Gravy	½ oz. gelatine

Cut the meat into neat pieces and the cooked forcemeat balls into quarters. Warm the gravy with the redcurrant jelly and add gelatine dissolved in a little hot water. When cold, but not set, stir in meat and forcemeat and pour into a well-moistened mould to set. If a full recipe of Jugged Hare is rather large for a family, it is useful to prepare this secondary dish at the same time. It is delicious served with a winter salad of celery and watercress.

Pack after unmoulding in heavy-duty foil.

To serve: Thaw in refrigerator for 6 hours or at room temperature for 3 hours.

Storage time: 1 month.

JUGGED HARE

1 hare	Salt and pepper
1 carrot	4 pints water
1 onion	2 oz. butter
1 blade mace	2 tbsp oil
Parsley, thyme and	1 tbsp cornflour
bay leaf	½ pint port
4 cloves	

Soak head, heart and liver of hare for 1 hour in cold salted water. Put into a pan with carrot, onion, mace, herbs, cloves, salt and pepper and water, and simmer for 3 hours, skimming frequently. Coat pieces of hare lightly in seasoned flour and brown in mixture of butter and oil. Put into a casserole. Strain stock and mix with cornflour blended with a little water. Simmer until reduced to 3 pints and pour over hare. Cover and cook at 325°F (Gas Mark 3) for 4 hours. Remove hare pieces and cool. Add port to gravy and simmer until of coating consistency. Cool.

Pack in waxed or rigid plastic containers, covering with gravy, and leaving ¾ in. headspace.

To serve: Put into casserole and heat at 350°F (Gas Mark 4) for 45 minutes, adding fresh or frozen forcemeat balls 10 minutes before serving time.

Storage time: 1 month.

FORCEMEAT BALLS

2 oz. suet	1 tsp chopped thyme
4 oz. fresh white breadcrumbs	Grated rind of ½ lemon
2 tsp chopped parsley	Salt and pepper
	1 medium egg

Grate suet and mix all ingredients together, binding with the egg. Freeze uncooked or deep-fried in balls.

Pack uncooked stuffing into cartons or polythene bags. Cooked forcemeat balls may be packed in cartons or bags.

To serve: Thaw stuffing enough to form into balls, deep-fry and add to casseroles or jugged hare. Put frozen ready-cooked balls into casserole 10 minutes before serving time.

Storage time: 1 month.

BEEF GALANTINE

12 oz. minced fresh beef	3 oz. shredded suet
2 oz. fresh white breadcrumbs	Salt and pepper
1 medium onion	1 tsp mixed herbs
	1 egg

Grate the onion, and mix together all ingredients, binding with the egg. Form into a neat roll or oblong. Dip a cloth in boiling water, flour well, and put the galantine in this. Steam for 2¾ hours. Unwrap the cloth and cool galantine completely.

Pack galantine in freezer paper, heavy-duty foil or polythene.

To serve: Thaw in refrigerator for 6 hours, or at room temperature for 3 hours. Roll galantine in crisp breadcrumbs.

Storage time: 1 month.

SCALLOPS WITH MUSHROOMS

8 scallops	4 oz. butter
½ pint dry white wine	Juice of 1 lemon
1 small onion	4 oz. small mushrooms
Parsley, thyme and bay leaf	1 tbsp plain flour
	Salt and pepper
	2 oz. grated cheese

Clean scallops and put in a pan with wine, chopped onion and herbs. Simmer 5 minutes, no longer as they become tough, and drain scallops, keeping liquid. Melt half the butter, add lemon juice and cook sliced mushrooms until just soft. Drain mushrooms. Add remaining butter to pan, work in flour, and pour in liquid from scallops. Simmer for 2 minutes. Season with salt and pepper and add grated cheese. Cut scallops in pieces, mix with mushrooms and a little sauce, and divide between 8 scallop shells or individual dishes. Coat with remaining sauce. If liked, pipe edges with creamed potato.

Pack by putting shells on to trays, freezing, then wrapping in foil.

To serve: Heat frozen scallops at 400°F (Gas Mark 6) for 20 minutes, after sprinkling surface with a few buttered breadcrumbs which may also be frozen.

Storage time: 1 month.

FISH CAKES

1 lb cooked white fish	2 oz. butter
1 lb mashed potato	Salt and pepper
4 tsp chopped parsley	2 small eggs

Mix flaked fish, potato, parsley, melted butter and seasonings together and bind with egg. Divide the mixture into sixteen pieces and form into flat rounds. Coat with egg and breadcrumbs and fry until golden. Cool quickly.

Pack in polythene bags or waxed cartons, separating fish cakes with waxed paper or Cellophane. Fish cakes may also be frozen uncovered on baking sheets and packed when solid.

To serve: Reheat in oven or frying-pan with a little fat, allowing 5 minutes' cooking on each side.

Storage time: 1 month.

BASIC PANCAKES

4 oz. plain flour	½ pint milk
¼ tsp salt	1 tbsp oil or melted butter
1 egg and 1 egg yolk	

Sift flour and salt and mix in egg and egg yolk and a little milk. Work together and gradually add remaining milk, beating to a smooth batter. Fold in oil or melted butter. Fry large or small thin pancakes. Pancakes may be frozen for use with savoury or sweet fillings. They can also be filled and frozen ready for use, with or without a suitable sauce. Fillings which can be frozen include creamed chicken and mushrooms; prawns or lobster in cream sauce; sweetbreads, chicken livers or ham in wine sauce; creamed smoked haddock; spinach and cheese. The filled pancakes can be covered with a mushroom, cheese or wine sauce before freezing, or finished with a sauce or grated cheese at the reheating stage.

Pack unfilled pancakes in layers separated by Cellophane, and put in foil or polythene bag.

To serve: Separate the pancakes, put on a baking sheet and cover with foil, and heat at 400°F (Gas Mark 6) for 10 minutes.

Storage time: 2 months.

APRICOT AND ALMOND PUDDING

8 oz. dried apricots
8 oz. self-raising flour
½ tsp salt
½ tsp bicarbonate of soda
½ tsp baking powder
4 oz. shredded suet
1 oz. sugar
Few drops almond essence
4 tbsp golden syrup

Soak apricots overnight in water to cover. Put 1 tbsp syrup in bottom of 1 quart foil pudding basin. Sift flour, salt, bicarbonate of soda and baking powder, and add suet, sugar and essence. Mix to a firm paste with water drained from the apricots. Divide pastry into three pieces and roll into rounds to fit basin. Put a layer of apricots, cut side down, on the bottom, then put a piece of pastry in basin. Cover with more syrup, apricots and pastry and then repeat layers, finishing with pastry. Cover with foil and steam for 2 hours. Cool completely.

Pack by putting a new piece of foil over pudding basin.

To serve: Steam for 1 hour, and serve with hot apricot jam and chopped blanched almonds.

Storage time: 2 months.

STEAMED LEMON PUDDING

2 oz. butter or margarine	Pinch of salt
2 oz. caster sugar	Rind and juice of 1 lemon
4 oz. self-raising flour	2 eggs
	A little milk

Cream fat and sugar, and add flour, salt and lemon rind and juice. Mix with beaten eggs and if necessary a little milk, to give a soft dropping consistency. Put into 1 pint foil pudding basin and steam for 1 hour. Cool completely.

Pack by covering basin with foil lid.

To serve: Steam for 1 hour and serve with lemon curd.

Storage time: 2 months.

WHOLEMEAL FRUIT SCONES

4 oz. plain wholemeal flour	1½ oz. butter or margarine
2 tsp baking powder	½ oz. sugar
4 oz. plain white flour	1 oz. dried fruit
½ tsp salt	¼ pint milk

Sieve flours, baking powder and salt, and rub in fat. Mix with sugar and fruit and mix to a soft dough with milk. Roll out ½ in. thick and cut out with 2-in. cutter. Brush over with egg or milk and bake at 450°F (Gas Mark 8) for 10 minutes. Cool on a rack.

in a polythene bag.

rve: Thaw at room temperature for 30 minutes, or reheat in a moderate oven for 15 minutes, then split and butter.

Storage time: 2 months.

CHOCOLATE CAKE

4 oz. margarine	1 tbsp cocoa
5 oz. caster sugar	2 eggs
4 oz. self-raising flour	1 tbsp milk

Slightly soften margarine, put all ingredients into a bowl and blend until creamy and smooth. Bake in two 7-in. tins at 350°F (Gas Mark 4) for 30 minutes. Cool and fill with icing made by blending together 6 oz. icing sugar, 1 oz. cocoa, 2 oz. margarine and 2 dsp hot water. Fill and put layers together and put more icing on top of cake.

Pack in polythene bag or foil. It is easier to freeze the cake without wrapping, then pack for storage.

To serve: Remove from wrappings and thaw at room temperature for 3 hours.

Storage time: 4 months.

CHOCOLATE CRUMB CAKE

4 oz. butter	1 tbsp golden syrup
1 tbsp sugar	8 oz. fine biscuit
2 tbsp cocoa	crumbs

Cream butter and sugar and add cocoa and syrup. Mix well and blend in biscuit crumbs. Press mixture into greased foil tray about 1 in. deep.

Pack by covering foil tray with foil lid.

To serve: Remove foil lid and thaw at room temperature for 3 hours, then top with 2 oz. melted plain chocolate, leave to set and cut in small squares.

Storage time: 4 months.

BUN LOAF

12 oz. self-raising flour	2 oz. sultanas
1 tsp mixed spice	2 oz. stoned raisins
¼ tsp salt	1 oz. chopped peel
4½ oz. butter or margarine	½ oz. chopped walnuts
4 oz. caster sugar	1 egg
4 oz. currants	3 tbsp marmalade
	¼ pint milk

Sieve flour, spice and salt, and rub in butter or margarine. Stir in sugar, dried fruit, walnuts and marmalade. Beat the egg, add to the milk and stir into the other ingredients. Beat well and put mixture into greased and lined 2-lb loaf tin. Bake at 325°F (Gas Mark 3) for 2 hours. Cool on a rack.

Pack in foil or a polythene bag.

To serve: Thaw at room temperature for 3 hours.

Storage time: 4 months.

33

COFFEE KISSES

6 oz. self-raising flour
Pinch of salt
3 oz. butter or margarine
2 oz. caster sugar
1 egg yolk
1 tsp coffee essence

Icing:
2 oz. butter
3 oz. icing sugar
1 tsp coffee essence

Sift flour and salt, rub in butter or margarine, and stir in sugar. Mix to a stiff paste with the egg yolk and coffee essence. Shape into 24 small balls and put on a greased baking tray. Bake at 375°F (Gas Mark 5) for 15 minutes. Cool on a rack. Mix icing by gradually beating together butter, icing sugar and coffee essence until soft and fluffy. Sandwich 'kisses' together in pairs.

Pack in box or polythene bag.

To serve: Thaw at room temperature for 1 hour, and dust with icing sugar.

Storage time: 2 months.

MARCH

This is the beginning of Spring, with the first salmon, English lamb, duckling, and a few early vegetables. It is still rather early to start freezing these raw materials which may not be available in large quantities, so this is a good month to cook ahead for school holidays and Easter, and to buy quick-cooking convenience foods for children's meals.

FOOD IN SEASON

Vegetables   Broccoli, Brussels sprouts, cabbage, cauliflower, celery, parsnips.
Fruit   Early rhubarb
Fish   Mackerel, oysters, salmon, scallops, whitebait.
Meat, Poultry and Game   Spring lamb, duckling.

BULK BUYING CHECKLIST

Fish fingers, beefburgers, chips, peas, ice cream, pasties, sausage rolls.

NOW IS THE TIME TO FREEZE:

*Broccoli, oysters, salmon, scallops, whitebait,
duckling*

BROCCOLI

Broccoli for freezing should have compact
heads with tender stalks not more than 1 in.
thick, and the heads should be uniformly
coloured. Discard any woody stems and trim
off outer leaves. Wash very thoroughly and
soak stems in a salt solution (2 tsp salt to 8
pints water) to get rid of insects. After 30
minutes, wash stems in clean water. Cut
broccoli into sprigs and blanch 3 minutes for
thin stems, 4 minutes for medium stems and 5
minutes for thick stems. Pack into bags or
boxes (if using boxes, alternate heads). *To
serve:* Cook 8 minutes in boiling water. *Storage
time:* 1 year.

SCALLOPS

Fresh scallops should be carefully washed and
opened and thoroughly cleaned. After washing
in salt water (1 tsp salt to 1 pint water), the fish
should be packed in water in cartons, and
should be completely covered, allowing $\frac{1}{2}$ in.
headspace. Scallops should be cooked after
freezing. Scallops tend to develop an oily taste
under freezer conditions. *Storage time:* 1
month.

WHITEBAIT

Wash and wipe fish thoroughly, and pack in
polythene bags in $\frac{1}{2}$ or 1 lb quantities. Thaw
out of container in the refrigerator, and wipe
dry before tossing in flour and frying. *Storage
time:* 4 months.

OYSTERS

Oysters should be washed in salt water and opened carefully, retaining the juice. Wash fish in salt water, allowing a proportion of 1 tsp salt to 1 pint water. Pack into cartons, covering with own juice, and seeing that the fish are completely covered. Allow $\frac{1}{2}$ in. headspace in cartons, and seal. Use either raw or cooked, immediately after thawing in container in the refrigerator. *Storage time:* 1 month.

SALMON

Freshly caught salmon must be well cleaned, the scales rubbed, and the fins removed. Small fish can be left whole, but larger ones are better divided into steaks. The fish should be washed well to remove blood and membranes, but salt water should not be used on salmon, which is a fatty fish. Separate pieces of fish with double thickness Cellophane, wrap in moisture-vapour-proof paper, carton or bag, seal and freeze. Be sure the paper is in close contact with the fish to exclude air which will dry the fish and make it tasteless. Freeze quickly in the coldest part of the freezer. *Storage time:* 4 months.

For a party, a large salmon is best protected by 'glazing'. Clean the fish, then place it *unwrapped* against the freezer wall in the coldest part of the freezer. When the fish is frozen solid, dip very quickly into very cold water so that a thin coating of ice will form. Return fish to freezer for an hour, and repeat the process. Continue until ice has built up to $\frac{1}{4}$ in. thickness. The fish can be stored without wrappings for 2 weeks, but is better wrapped in freezer paper for longer storage.

DUCKLING

The best ducks for freezing should be young, with pliable breastbones and flexible beaks. Ducklings may be frozen between 6 and 12 weeks, while older ducks between 3 and 7 lb weight are suitable. Ducks should be completely prepared for cooking, before freezing, and giblets and liver should be packaged separately as they have a short freezer storage life.

The birds should be starved for 24 hours before killing, and they should be plucked while still warm. After removing head, feet and innards, wipe the birds carefully inside and out with a damp cloth. It is particularly important to see that the oil glands of ducks are removed before freezing. Chill the birds well, and wrap any protruding bones in foil or greaseproof paper before packing. *To serve:* Thaw 5-lb bird overnight in the refrigerator in unopened wrappings (the bird will take about 4 hours at room temperature). *Storage time:* 6–8 months.

PREPARE-AHEAD DISHES

CHICKEN LIVER PÂTÉ

8 oz. chicken livers	1 small onion
3 oz. fat bacon	1 egg
2 crushed garlic cloves	Salt and pepper

Cut livers in small pieces and cut up bacon and onion. Cook bacon and onion in a little butter until onion is just soft. Add livers and cook gently for 10 minutes. Mince very finely and season. Add garlic and beaten egg and put mixture into foil containers. Stand containers in a baking tin of water and cook at 350°F (Gas Mark 4) for 1 hour. Cool completely.

Pack by covering containers with heavy-duty foil.

To serve: Thaw at room temperature for 1 hour. Use immediately after thawing.

Storage time: 1 month.

DUCKLING PÂTÉ

4-lb duckling	Pinch of ground nutmeg
Duck liver	
8 oz. lean pork	3 tbsp dry white wine
4 oz. streaky bacon	
1 garlic clove	1 tbsp dry sherry
Pinch of ground mace	Salt and pepper

Roast the duck lightly and then mince the duck meat with the liver and pork twice. Line a terrine or loaf tin with the streaky bacon (make this very thin by flattening it out with a wide-bladed knife). Mix this meat with all other ingredients and pack into the terrine. Cover with a lid or foil and stand in a roasting tin with 1 in. of water. Cook at 300°F (Gas

Mark 2) for $1\frac{1}{2}$ hours, or until the mixture shrinks from the side of the dish. Cool under weights.

Pack by turning pâté out of terrine or tin and wrapping in heavy-duty foil.

To serve: Thaw at room temperature for 3 hours and serve with toast and crisp lettuce.

DUCK WITH PORT

5-lb duck	Salt and pepper
2 thick slices white bread	2 medium onions
Milk	1 large wineglass port
1 heaped tsp sage	1 lemon
1 tbsp chopped onion	

Wipe the duck inside and out and season with salt and pepper. Soak the bread (without crusts) in the milk, then squeeze out the liquid. Mix the crumbs with sage, onion, salt and pepper and a little grated orange peel if liked. Stuff the duck. Simmer the giblets in water to cover to make stock. Strain and add the onions chopped finely, and simmer until onions are just soft, and there is about $\frac{1}{2}$ pint gravy. Put duck in a casserole with this gravy and cook at 325°F (Gas Mark 3) for $1\frac{1}{2}$ hours, adding port about 15 minutes before cooking time finishes, and adding juice of the lemon when the casserole is removed from the heat. Cool completely.

Pack in container, covering duck with gravy.

To serve: Return to casserole and heat at 350°F (Gas Mark 4) for 1 hour; garnish with triangles of fried bread, and serve the gravy separately.

Storage time: 1 month.

NORMANDY RABBIT

1 young rabbit
3 oz. butter
4 cloves garlic

1 tbsp tomato purée
½ pint cider
Salt and pepper

Clean and joint the rabbit and simmer for 30 minutes, with a little salt and pepper. Remove meat from bones in large neat pieces, and fry the rabbit with the garlic cloves until golden. Stir in tomato purée, and season with salt and pepper. Simmer for 2 minutes, then pour on cider. Simmer for 5 minutes and cool.

Pack in container, covering rabbit pieces with sauce.

To serve: Reheat gently in double boiler and serve garnished with chopped parsley.

Storage time: 1 month.

LAMB CROQUETTES

8 oz. cooked lamb
3 tbsp butter
1 tbsp plain flour
4 fl. oz. milk
Pinch of paprika
Pinch of pepper
Pinch of nutmeg
¼ tsp salt
4 fl. oz. stock

1 tbsp chopped
   parsley
1 tbsp lemon juice
1 tbsp chopped
   onion
1 beaten egg
3 oz. dry white
   breadcrumbs

Mince the lamb. Melt butter, blend in flour and add milk and stock. Cook and stir all the time until mixture thickens and is smooth. Add seasonings, parsley, lemon juice and onion. Add the meat and chill. Shape mixture into cones, roll in egg and breadcrumbs, and fry in deep fat until golden brown. Cool.

Pack in container, or in polythene bag.

To serve: Reheat at 350°F (Gas Mark 4) for

30 minutes, and serve with peas in a white sauce.

Storage time: 1 month.

LAMB PIES

1 lb lean lamb	2 tbsp plain flour
3 medium onions	2 tbsp chopped
1 tsp salt	parsley
Good pinch of	8 oz. short pastry
pepper	

Cut meat into small pieces, and chop onions. Put meat, onions and seasoning into a pan and just cover with water. Simmer with lid on until meat is tender. Blend flour with a little cold water and use to thicken gravy. Add parsley and cool. Line small patty tins with pastry and put a little mixture in each tin. Cover with pastry lids, seal edges, cut a small slit in the top of each, and brush with egg or milk. Bake at 400°F (Gas Mark 6) for 25 minutes. Cool completely.

Pack in carton or polythene bag.

To serve: Thaw completely at room temperature for 2 hours to eat cold, or reheat in low oven to serve hot.

Storage time: 1 month.

SEA PIE

4 oz. short pastry	½ pint milk
8 oz. cooked cod or	1 oz. plain flour
haddock	1 oz. butter
4 oz. prawns or	3 oz. grated cheese
shrimps	Salt and pepper

Line 9-in. pie plate or foil dish with pastry and bake blind for 15 minutes. Flake fish and prepare prawns or shrimps if fresh. Melt butter, add flour and cook gently for 1 minute. Stir in milk, and bring to the boil, stirring all the time. Add fish, prawns or shrimps, cheese and seasonings. Cool slightly and pour into pastry case. Bake at 400°F (Gas Mark 6) for 20 minutes. Cool completely.

Pack in polythene bag, heavy-duty foil, or carton to avoid crushing.

To serve: Thaw at room temperature for 2 hours to eat cold, or reheat at 325°F (Gas Mark 3) for 30 minutes to eat hot.

Storage time: 1 month.

RHUBARB CREAM

1 lb early rhubarb	6 oz. sugar
½ pint water	2 tbsp cornflour

Cut rhubarb in pieces. Bring water to boil, add rhubarb and sugar and boil until fruit is soft. Mix cornflour with a little water, blend into hot liquid and bring back to boil. Cool.

Pack in rigid plastic or waxed container.

To serve: Thaw in refrigerator for 1 hour and serve with cream.

Storage time: 1 month.

RHUBARB COMPÔTE

1 lb early rhubarb	Sugar to taste
4 oz. marmalade	

Cut rhubarb into neat pieces and put into a pan with the marmalade and just enough water to prevent burning. Cook gently until fruit is soft but not broken. Sweeten to taste and cool.

Pack in rigid plastic or waxed container.

To serve: Thaw in refrigerator for 1 hour and serve with very thick cream.

Storage time: 6 months.

MARMALADE PUDDING

2 oz. fresh white breadcrumbs	2 oz. butter
8 oz. marmalade	¼ pint milk
	1 egg

Put breadcrumbs and marmalade in a basin and pour over butter heated with milk. Mix well and add beaten egg. Turn into a greased foil pudding basin and steam for 2½ hours. Cool completely.

Pack by covering basin with heavy-duty foil lid, or by putting basin in a polythene bag.

To serve: Steam for 1 hour and serve with cream or custard.

Storage time: 2 months.

LEMON CRUMB PUDDING

8 oz. white breadcrumbs	Grated rind and juice of 1 lemon
4 oz. butter or margarine	Apricot jam or pineapple jam
4 oz. sugar	

Mix together crumbs, softened butter, sugar, and lemon juice and rind. Spread jam liberally in the bottom of an oven dish which can be used in the freezer, or in a foil pie dish. Put on mixture and bake at 350°F (Gas Mark 4) for 30 minutes. Cool completely.

Pack by putting basin in polythene bag, or by covering dish with heavy-duty foil lid.

To serve: Heat at 325°F (Gas Mark 3) for 30 minutes, and serve with cream or custard.

Storage time: 2 months.

HOT CROSS BUNS

1 lb plain flour
Pinch of salt
½ pint milk and
water mixed
½ oz. yeast
2 oz. caster sugar
2 oz. butter

3 oz. currants
1 oz. chopped
candied peel
1 tsp cinnamon
1 tsp nutmeg
1 egg

Put half the flour in a bowl. Mix yeast with a little of the milk and water which should be just warm, and whisk in remaining liquid. Pour into flour and mix well. Cover with a damp cloth and leave in a warm place for 40 minutes. Mix together remaining flour, salt, cinnamon, nutmeg and sugar and stir in fruit. Melt butter and beat up the egg. Add all the dry ingredients to the yeast mixture, and pour in butter and egg, then mix thoroughly with the hands. Return to bowl, cover with damp cloth, and leave for 1 hour in a warm place. Divide dough into 16 pieces and shape each piece into a round. Put on a greased and floured baking tray, leaving room for buns to spread. Make a cross using a knife on each bun, or put on a cross made from narrow strips of pastry. Leave in a warm place for 40 minutes, then bake at 425°F (Gas Mark 7) for 20 minutes. Five minutes before removing from the oven, brush over with milk and sugar. Cool on a rack.

Pack in polythene bags.

To serve: Thaw at room temperature for 1 hour. Reheat in a low oven to serve warm.

Storage time: 2 months.

PRUNE CAKE

5 oz. butter or margarine	2 eggs
5 oz. sugar	6 oz. prunes
Grated rind of 1 lemon	8 oz. plain flour
	1 tsp baking powder

Cream the fat and sugar until light and soft. Add lemon rind and beat in the eggs. Chop the prunes finely and add to the mixture with sieved flour and baking powder. Add a little milk if needed to give a soft consistency. Put into 7-in. round tin which has been greased and lined. Bake at 325°F (Gas Mark 3) for 1½ hours. Cool on rack.

Pack in polythene bag or in heavy-duty foil.

To serve: Thaw at room temperature for 3 hours and dust with icing sugar.

Storage time: 2 months.

POUND CAKE

8 oz. plain flour	4 oz. currants
Pinch of salt	4 oz. sultanas
8 oz. butter or margarine	4 oz. candied peel
8 oz. caster sugar	2 oz. chopped almonds
4 eggs	½ wineglass brandy
Grated rind of 2 lemons	

Sieve flour and salt. Cream fat until soft, add sugar and beat until light and fluffy. Add eggs one at a time with a little flour, beating well after each addition. Add brandy with a little more flour. Stir in remaining flour, lemon rind and fruit. Put mixture into greased and lined 8-in. tin, and hollow out centre. Bake at 300°F (Gas Mark 2) for 2¾ hours. Cool on a rack.

Pack in polythene bag or in heavy-duty foil.

To serve: Thaw at room temperature for 3 hours.

Storage time: 2 months.

APRICOT ALMOND TARTS

6 oz. short pastry	1 large egg white
Apricot jam	Almond essence
2 oz. caster sugar	1 tbsp cold water
1 oz. ground almonds	

Line 12 tartlet tins with pastry, and cut 24 small strips to decorate the tops of the tarts. Put a spoonful of jam in each pastry case. Mix together sugar and almonds. Whisk egg white until stiff and stir in almond mixture and a little almond essence. Add enough water to make the mixture slack. Half fill the pastry cases and put pastry crosses on top. Bake at 425°F (Gas Mark 7) for 12 minutes.

Pack in boxes to avoid crushing.

To serve: Thaw at room temperature for 2 hours.

Storage time: 2 months.

APRIL

An unpredictable month, and it is still too early for much preservation, except for broccoli and spinach. Shop pineapples are good value, and English lamb is in good supply. This is a good time to keep a supply of bread and cakes in the freezer for the first outdoor expeditions and picnics.

FOOD IN SEASON

Vegetables Broccoli, Brussels sprouts, parsnips, spinach.
Fruit Pineapple, rhubarb.
Fish Crab, mackerel, prawns, salmon, trout, whitebait.
Meat, Poultry and Game Spring lamb, duckling, guinea fowl.

WHAT TO BUY FROM THE SHOPS

Bread (including baps and rolls), fruit bread.

BULK BUYING CHECKLIST

Fish fingers, beefburgers, chips, peas, ice-cream, pasties, sausage rolls.

NOW IS THE TIME TO FREEZE:

Spinach, pineapple, prawns, trout, guinea fowl, bread

SPINACH

Choose young tender spinach without heavy leaf ribs. Remove stems and any bruised or discoloured leaves. Wash very thoroughly. Blanch for 2 minutes, moving the container so the leaves separate. Cool quickly and press out excess moisture with a wooden spoon. Pack in rigid containers, leaving $\frac{1}{2}$ in. headspace, or in polythene bags. *To serve:* Cook 7 minutes in a little melted butter. *Storage time:* 1 year.

PINEAPPLE

Pineapple freezes very well indeed, if the fruit is ripe, with golden yellow flesh. Peel the fruit and cut into slices or chunks. Freeze in dry unsweetened packs, using double thickness of Cellophane to keep slices separate. Pineapple may also be frozen in 30% syrup (7 oz. sugar to 1 pint water), including any pineapple juice which has resulted from the preparation. Crushed pineapple can be packed with sugar, using 4 oz. sugar to each 2 breakfast cups of prepared fruit. *To serve:* Thaw at room temperature for 3 hours. *Storage time:* 1 year.

PRAWNS

Freshly caught prawns should be cooked and cooled in the cooking water. Remove shells, pack tightly in bags or cartons, leaving ½ in. headspace, seal and freeze. Prawns may be frozen in their shells with heads removed, but there is no advantage in this method as they must later be prepared for use before serving. *To serve:* Thaw in unopened wrappings in a refrigerator, allowing 6 hours for 1-lb or 1-pint package. Prawns may be added to cooked dishes while still frozen, and heated through. *Storage time:* 1 month.

TROUT

Clean freshly caught trout thoroughly and remove fins. Pack singly in moisture-vapour-proof paper, carton or polythene bag, seal and freeze. Be sure the paper is in close contact with the fish to exclude air which will dry the fish and make it tasteless. Freeze quickly in the coldest part of the freezer. *Storage time:* 4 months.

GUINEA FOWL

Prepare the bird ready for cooking, being sure there is no skin damage. Pad any protruding bones with a small piece of paper or foil to avoid tearing freezer wrappings. Pack in polythene bag, removing all air. *To serve:* Thaw overnight in refrigerator in wrappings. Young birds may be roasted with a stuffing (use one suitable for chicken), but need extra butter and bacon to keep them moist during cooking. Older birds are better casseroled. *Storage time:* 8–12 months.

BREAD

It is practical to keep bread in the freezer during holiday months ready for days when shops may be shut, or a picnic is needed. Wrap in heavy-duty foil or polythene for storage. *To serve:* Thaw in wrappings at room temperature A 1½-lb loaf will take about 3 hours. Bread can be quickly thawed in foil in the oven (400°F or Gas Mark 6) for 45 minutes, but will quickly stale after thawing. Sliced bread can be separated carefully with a knife while still frozen, and used immediately for toasting, or thawed for sandwiches. *Storage time:* 4 weeks (white and brown loaves); 6 weeks (enriched bread and rolls made with milk, fruit bread, malt loaves and soft rolls); 1 week (crusted loaves and rolls).

Part-baked rolls and loaves

These items bought from the shops are also useful in the holidays. Leave rolls and loaves in the polythene bags in which they are sold, but put into a second bag in case the shop wrapping has been punctured. *To serve:* Place frozen unwrapped loaf in a hot oven (425°F or Gas Mark 7) for 30 minutes. Cool for 1–2 hours before cutting. Rolls should be placed in a fairly hot oven (400°F or Gas Mark 6) for 15 minutes. *Storage time:* 4 months.

DUCK IN CIDER SAUCE

4-lb duck	3 oz. butter
8 oz. cooking apples	¾ pint cider
2 oz. breadcrumbs	3 tsp cornflour
Rind and juice of	
1 orange	

Wipe inside and outside duck. Melt butter in a frying-pan and fry crumbs lightly. Add chopped apples and grated orange rind, and fry until cooked. Stuff bird with this mixture. Prick duck with a fork, and put on its side in a roasting tin. Cook at 325°F (Gas Mark 3) for ½ hour. Strain off fat and turn so backbone is uppermost. Pour over cider and orange juice and cook ½ hour. Turn bird so breast is uppermost and cook for ½ hour. Blend cornflour with a little water, add hot cider and bird juices and boil for 2 minutes. Pour over duck. Cool completely.

Pack in waxed or rigid plastic container, making sure sauce covers duck.

To serve: Heat at 325°F (Gas Mark 3) for 1 hour. The dish may also be eaten cold if thawed at room temperature for 3 hours, and served with a fresh orange salad.

Storage time: 1 month.

CHICKEN PIE

5-lb boiling chicken	1 lb carrots
2 celery stalks	2 lb shelled peas
1 medium onion	6 oz. mushrooms
½ sliced lemon	½ pint thin cream
2 sprigs parsley	Pinch of nutmeg
1 bay leaf	2 oz. cornflour
Salt and pepper	2 lb flaky pastry

Simmer chicken in water for 2½ hours with celery, onion, lemon, parsley, bay leaf, salt and pepper. Cool chicken in stock and cut flesh from bones in neat cubes. Slice carrots and cook carrots and peas for 5 minutes (frozen vegetables may be used if fresh ones are not available). Cook sliced mushrooms in a little butter. Drain vegetables and mix with chicken flesh. Measure out 2 pints of chicken stock and make a sauce with cornflour, a seasoning of nutmeg, salt and pepper to taste, and stir in the thin cream without boiling. Simmer for 3 minutes until smooth, pour over chicken mixture and cool completely. Divide mixture into foil pie plates and cover with flaky pastry. This quantity of filling will make eight 6-in.-diameter pies.

Pack by wrapping containers in foil or polythene bags.

To serve: Cut slits in pastry and put dishes on baking sheet. Bake at 450°F (Gas Mark 8) for 40 minutes.

Storage time: 2 months.

ROYAL CHICKEN

8 chicken pieces	1 gill stock
4 oz. bacon	Bay leaf, thyme and
2 oz. butter	parsley
4 small onions	Salt and pepper
4 oz. mushrooms	1 tbsp flour
½ pint red wine	

Wipe the chicken joints. Cut bacon into dice. Melt half the butter and fry the onions until golden, then the bacon and chicken. Add sliced mushrooms, stock, herbs, salt and pepper, cover and cook slowly until the chicken is tender. Take out chicken and mushrooms and keep hot. Skim fat from gravy, and stir in wine. Melt remaining butter, add flour and stir. Add the chicken gravy and simmer until creamy and smooth. Pour over chicken and cool completely.

Pack in waxed or rigid plastic container, making sure chicken pieces are covered in sauce.

To serve: Put into casserole and heat at 325°F (Gas Mark 4) for 1 hour.

Storage time: 1 month.

BEEF OLIVES

1½ lb buttock steak	2 oz. suet
1½ oz. plain flour	2 oz. bacon
Salt and pepper	4 oz. breadcrumbs
2 oz. dripping	Rind of ½ lemon
1 carrot	¼ tsp mixed herbs
2 small onions	1 egg
1 pint stock	

Cut steak into pieces about 2 × 3 in., and flatten well. Make a stuffing with suet, chopped bacon, breadcrumbs, lemon rind, herbs, salt and pepper to taste, and bind with beaten egg. Spread this mixture on the steak pieces and tie up with cotton or fine string. Season flour with salt and pepper, and toss beef rolls in this. Heat dripping and fry meat rolls lightly, then remove from fat. Fry diced carrot and sliced onion until golden, and work in any remaining flour. Add stock and test seasoning. Put in beef olives and simmer gently for 1¼ hours. Cool completely.

Pack in waxed or rigid plastic containers, making sure gravy covers meat.

To serve: Reheat at 325°F (Gas Mark 3) for 1 hour and sprinkle with chopped parsley.

Storage time: 1 month.

COTTAGE PIE

1 lb cooked beef or lamb	1 medium onion
¼ pint stock	1 lb mashed potato
	Salt and pepper

This recipe may be made with fresh minced meat, but in most households is prepared from left-over roast meat. Mince the meat and moisten with stock, seasoning to taste. Mix with the onion which has been chopped and lightly cooked in a little fat. Put into foil container and cover with mashed potato. Reconstituted mashed potato powder can be used with good results.

Pack foil container in polythene bag, or cover with a lid of heavy-duty foil.

To serve: Put in cold oven and reheat at 400°F (Gas Mark 6) for 45 minutes.

Storage time: 1 month.

MEAT BALLS

¾ lb minced fresh
  beef
¼ lb minced fresh
  pork
2 oz. dry white
  breadcrumbs

½ pint creamy milk
1 small chopped
  onion
1½ tsp salt
¼ tsp pepper
Butter

Mix together beef and pork and soak breadcrumbs in milk. Cook onion in a little butter
until golden, and mix together with meat,
breadcrumbs and seasonings until well blended. Shape into 1-in. balls, using 2 tbsp dipped
in cold water. Fry balls in butter until evenly
browned, shaking pan to keep balls round.
Cook a few at a time, draining each batch, and
cool.

Pack in bags, or in boxes with greaseproof
paper between layers.

To serve: Thaw in wrappings in refrigerator
for 3 hours and eat cold. To serve hot, fry
quickly in hot fat, or heat in tomato sauce or
gravy.

Storage time: 1 month.

SALMON KEDGEREE

1 lb. cooked salmon
8 oz. Patna rice
3 oz. butter
Salt and pepper

1 tbsp chopped
  parsley
2 hard-boiled egg
  yolks

Flake the fish. Cook rice in fast-boiling salted
water for about 20 minutes until tender, and
drain well. Mix with flaked fish, melted butter,
seasonings, parsley and chopped egg yolks.
For a supper dish, 4 oz. chopped button
mushrooms cooked in a little butter may be
added.

Pack in foil container covered with lid of heavy-duty foil, or in polythene bag.

To serve: Thaw in refrigerator for 3 hours, then reheat in double saucepan over boiling water. The dish may be put into a cold oven straight from the freezer and heated at 400°F (Gas Mark 6) for 45 minutes. Heating will be speeded if the dish is stirred occasionally.

Storage time: 1 month.

SALMON TURNOVERS

8 oz. flaky pastry	4 tomatoes
8 oz. cooked salmon	1 tsp curry powder
1 oz. butter	Salt and pepper

Roll pastry into two 12-in. squares. Flake the fish and mix with melted butter, curry powder, salt and pepper. Divide mixture between two pieces of pastry. Skin tomatoes and cover fish mixture with tomato slices. Fold in corners of pastry to form envelope shapes and seal edges. Smoked haddock is also good for this dish.

Pack in foil or polythene bags.

To serve: Put frozen turnovers on tray and bake at 475°F (Gas Mark 9) for 20 minutes, then at 400°F (Gas Mark 6) for 20 minutes.

Storage time: 1 month.

RHUBARB CHARLOTTE

1½ lb rhubarb
4 oz. sugar
Grated rind and
  juice of 1 orange

8 oz. soft white
  breadcrumbs
3 oz. shredded suet

Cut rhubarb into small pieces and cook with sugar, orange rind and juice and very little water until tender. Mix breadcrumbs and suet together. Put a layer of crumb mixture into the bottom of a greased straight-sided dish and put into oven set at 350°F (Gas Mark 4) for 10 minutes. Remove dish from oven and put in alternate layers of rhubarb and crumbs, ending with crumbs. Bake for 1 hour. Turn out and cool completely.

Pack in heavy-duty foil or in rigid container.

To serve: Thaw in refrigerator for 6 hours to serve cold with cream. The pudding may be reheated at 350°F (Gas Mark 4) for 45 minutes to serve hot with cream or custard.

Storage time: 1 month.

GINGER WALNUT SPONGE

8 oz. plain flour
1 tsp cream of tartar
½ tsp bicarbonate of
  soda
3 oz. butter or
  margarine
3 oz. sugar

4 oz. chopped
  walnuts
2 tsp ground ginger
2 tbsp golden
  syrup
4 fl. oz. milk
1 small egg

Sieve the flour and cream of tartar and rub in the butter or margarine Dissolve the bicarbonate of soda in the milk, and add it with the rest of the ingredients to the flour. Mix thoroughly and bake in 7-in. square tin at 325°F (Gas Mark 3) for 1 hour.

Pack in polythene bag or foil. It is easier to freeze the cake without wrapping, then pack for freezing.

To serve: Remove from wrappings and thaw at room temperature for 3 hours.

Storage time: 4 months.

GOLDEN LEMON CAKE

1½ oz. butter	6 oz. self-raising
6 oz. caster sugar	flour
3 egg yolks	¼ pint milk
¼ tsp lemon essence	Pinch of salt

Cream butter and sugar until fluffy and slowly add egg yolks and lemon essence. Add flour alternately with milk and the pinch of salt. Bake in two 8-in. tins lined with paper at 350°F (Gas Mark 4) for 25 minutes. Cool, fill and ice with *Lemon Frosting*. Make this by blending together 3 tbsp butter, 1 tbsp grated orange rind, 2 tbsp lemon juice, 1 tbsp water and 1 lb icing sugar. This cake makes an excellent Easter cake if decorated with mimosa balls and angelica after defrosting.

Pack in polythene bag or foil. It is easier to freeze the cake without wrapping, then pack for storage.

To serve: Remove from wrappings and thaw at room temperature for 3 hours.

Storage time: 4 months.

BROWNIES

8 oz. granulated sugar	½ tsp salt
1½ oz. cocoa	2 eggs
3 oz. self-raising flour	2 tbsp creamy milk
	4 oz. melted butter or margarine

Stir together sugar, cocoa, flour and salt. Beat eggs and milk, and add to the dry mixture with melted fat. 3 oz. shelled walnuts or seedless raisins may be added if liked. Pour into 8 × 12-in. tin and bake at 350°F (Gas Mark 4) for 30 minutes. Cool in tin.

Pack by covering baking tin with foil, or by putting tin into polythene bag. A baking tin may be made of heavy-duty foil for cooking and freezing if a normal baking tin cannot be spared for storage.

To serve: Thaw in wrappings at room temperature for 3 hours, then top with 4 oz. melted plain chocolate.

Storage time: 4 months.

EASTER BISCUITS

8 oz. plain flour	3 oz. caster sugar
Pinch of salt	1 small beaten egg
½ tsp mixed spice	3 oz. currants
3 oz. butter or margarine	

Sieve flour, salt and spice. Cream fat and sugar until light and fluffy. Beat in a little egg and flour, then stir in currants and remaining flour, adding a little more egg if necessary to make a firm paste. Roll out thinly, cut into large rounds (with the top of a tumbler) and put on greased tray. Prick with a fork, brush over with milk and sprinkle with caster sugar.

Bake at 325°F (Gas Mark 3) for 20 minutes. Cool on a rack.

Pack in container to prevent crushing.

To serve: Thaw at room temperature for 1 hour.

Storage time: 2 months.

FREEZER FUDGE

4 oz. plain chocolate	1 lb sifted icing
4 oz. butter	sugar
1 egg	2 tbsp sweetened
	condensed milk

Melt chocolate and butter in a double saucepan over hot water. Beat egg lightly, mix with sugar and milk, and stir in the chocolate mixture. Turn into greased rectangular tin.

Pack by covering container with lid of heavy-duty foil. Freeze for 6 hours, cut in squares and pack in polythene bags. Store in freezer.

To serve: Leave at room temperature for 15 minutes.

Storage time: 3 months.

MAY

This is a good month to start freezing raw materials, with good supplies of early vegetables, English lamb and many fish.

FOOD IN SEASON

Vegetables Asparagus, broad beans, broccoli, carrots, cauliflower, peas, spinach.
Fruit Pineapple, rhubarb.
Fish Crab, herring, lobster, plaice, prawns, salmon, trout, whitebait.
Meat, Poultry and Game Spring lamb, duckling, guinea fowl.

NOW IS THE TIME TO FREEZE:

Asparagus, broad beans, carrots, peas, lobster, crab

ASPARAGUS

Asparagus should be frozen immediately after picking. Woody portions and small scales should be removed, and the asparagus washed thoroughly. Sort into small, medium and large heads, and blanch each size separately. Cut asparagus into 6-in. lengths, and allow 2 minutes for small spears, 3 minutes for medium spears and 4 minutes for large spears. Cool at once and drain thoroughly. Package in sizes, or in mixed bundles if preferred (it is better to pack in similar sizes so that cooking time can be carefully controlled). Pack in boxes lined with moisture-vapour-proof paper. Asparagus may also be made up into bundles alternating the heads, and wrapped in freezer paper. *To serve:* Plunge into boiling water and cook for 5 minutes. *Storage time:* 9 months.

BROAD BEANS

Broad beans for freezing should be small and young, with tender outer skins. Remove beans from shells, blanch for 1½ minutes, and pack in cartons or polythene bags. *To serve:* Put in boiling salted water for 8 minutes. *Storage time:* 1 year.

CARROTS

Only very young carrots should be frozen, and they should be washed thoroughly and scraped. They may be frozen whole, or sliced and diced, but cut-up ones will need $\frac{1}{2}$ in. headspace. Blanch whole carrots or sliced or diced carrots for 3 minutes and pack in polythene bags. *To serve:* Cook for 8 minutes in boiling water. *Storage time:* 1 year.

PEAS

Home-grown peas should be frozen when young and sweet, and old starchy ones should be avoided. They should be prepared for the freezer as soon as they have been gathered. Shell peas, and blanch for 1 minute, lifting the basket in and out of the water to distribute heat evenly through layers of peas. Chill immediately and pack in bags or rigid containers. *To serve:* Cook in boiling water for 7 minutes. *Storage time:* 1 year.

LOBSTER

Lobster should only be frozen if freshly caught. The fish should be cooked, cooled and split, and the flesh removed from the shells. Pack into bags or cartons, leaving $\frac{1}{2}$ in. headspace. It is possible to freeze cooked lobsters in the shell, but this may make later preparation more difficult. Lobster can also be frozen in a variety of prepared dishes, but suffers from the consequent overcooking. *To serve:* Thaw in refrigerator in container for 6 hours, and serve cold. *Storage time:* 1 month.

CRAB

Crab can be frozen if freshly caught and cooked. The crab should be cooked, drained and cooled thoroughly, and all edible meat removed. It is best packed in small containers, leaving $\frac{1}{2}$ in. headspace. *To serve:* Thaw in refrigerator in container, and serve very cold. *Storage time:* 1 month.

PREPARE-AHEAD DISHES

POTTED CRAB

8 oz. fresh crabmeat
4 oz. butter
1 tsp black pepper
1 tsp ground mace

Pinch of cayenne
  pepper
Juice of ½ lemon

Heat ½ oz. butter in a pan, and add pepper, mace and cayenne pepper. When butter is hot, add crab and lemon juice, and stir well until crab is hot but not brown. Pack into small waxed or plastic cartons. Heat the rest of the butter until it is foamy, skim, and pour over crab, covering it completely. Leave until butter is hard.

Pack by covering cartons with lids.

To serve: Thaw overnight in refrigerator, turn out, and serve with hot toast and lemon slices.

Storage time: 2 months.

FRESH SALMON PÂTÉ

1 lb fresh salmon
4 1-in. slices white
  bread (large loaf)
⅓ pint milk
1 oz. butter
1 egg yolk

2 tbsp chopped
  parsley
½ tsp salt
½ tsp pepper
Juice of ½ lemon

If this pâté proves useful and popular, it can be made at other times of the year with drained canned salmon, but it is advisable to reduce the quantity of salt when this is used.

Wrap the salmon in foil, cover with cold water, bring to the boil and simmer for 5 minutes. Remove from heat and leave fish in the water until cold. Remove crusts from bread, and break bread into pieces, then leave to soak in the milk. Flake salmon into a bowl, and mix in the soaked bread and milk which have been well mixed together. Add softened butter, egg yolk and parsley, and mix thoroughly with salt, pepper and lemon juice. Pack mixture in a serving dish which can be used in the oven and the freezer. Stand dish in a tin of water, and cook at 300°F (Gas Mark 4) for 1 hour. Leave until completely cold.

Pack by covering dish with lid of heavy-duty foil.

To serve: Thaw in refrigerator overnight, and serve with hot toast and lemon slices. This pâté is also excellent with salad, or in sandwiches.

Storage time: 2 months.

SUMMER GALANTINE

1 lb rump steak	3 oz. fresh white
8 oz. lean cooked	breadcrumbs
ham	2 eggs
1 medium onion	Salt and pepper
1 tbsp tomato purée	

Cut fat from steak and ham, and put through a mincer with the onion. Mince the mixture a second time. Mix together with tomato purée, breadcrumbs, eggs and seasoning to taste. Pack into 2-lb foil basin and steam for 4 hours. Cool under a weight.

Pack by putting foil basin into a polythene bag. If a china basin has been used, turn out galantine and wrap in heavy-duty foil or polythene.

To serve: Thaw in refrigerator for 6 hours and serve with salad or in sandwiches.

Storage time: 2 months.

QUICHE LORRAINE

4 oz. short pastry	1 egg and 1 egg yolk
½ oz. butter	2 oz. grated cheese
1 small onion	1 gill creamy milk
1 oz. streaky bacon	Pepper

Line a flan ring with pastry, or line a foil dish which can be put into the freezer. Gently soften chopped onion and bacon in butter until golden, and put into pastry case. Lightly beat together egg, egg yolk, cheese, milk and pepper. Add a little salt if the bacon is not very salty. Pour into flan case. Bake at 375°F (Gas Mark 5) for 30 minutes. Cool.

Pack in foil in rigid container to avoid breakage, and seal with freezer tape.

To serve: Thaw in refrigerator for 6 hours to serve cold. If preferred hot, heat at 350°F (Gas Mark 4) for 20 minutes.

Storage time: 2 months.

CHICKEN IN CURRY SAUCE

3 lb chicken pieces	1 tbsp vinegar
2 medium onions	1 tbsp brown sugar
1 tbsp curry powder	1 tbsp chutney
1 tbsp cornflour	1 tbsp sultanas
1 pint chicken stock (from cooking chicken pieces)	

Simmer chicken pieces in water until tender, drain off stock, and keep chicken warm. Fry sliced onions in a little butter until soft, add curry powder and cook for 1 minute. Slowly add chicken stock and the cornflour blended with a little water. Add remaining ingredients and simmer for 5 minutes. Add chicken pieces and simmer 15 minutes. Cool.

Pack in waxed or rigid plastic containers.
To serve: Heat in double boiler.
Storage time: 1 month.

DUCK WITH CHERRIES

4–5-lb duck	1 wineglass Madeira
2 oz. butter	or sherry
8 oz. black cherries	Salt and pepper
1 gill stock	1 dsp cherry brandy

Roast the duck with the butter inside. Remove duck from tin and pour off fat. Cut duck into large pieces. Put stoned cherries, stock, Madeira (or sherry), salt and pepper in the roasting tin, bring to the boil and simmer until cherries are tender. Remove from heat, stir in cherry brandy and pour over duck. Cool.

Pack into rigid plastic containers (cherry juice may leak through waxed containers).

To serve: Thaw at room temperature for 1 hour, and reheat in double boiler.

Storage time: 2 months.

BAKED CHEESECAKE

2 oz. digestive biscuit crumbs	1 tbsp cornflour
1 lb cottage cheese	2 tbsp double cream
1 tsp lemon juice	2 eggs
1 tsp grated orange rind	4 oz. caster sugar

Use an 8-in. cake tin with removable base to bake this cheesecake. Butter sides and line base with buttered paper. Sprinkle with crumbs. Sieve cottage cheese and mix with lemon juice, orange rind and cornflour. Whip cream and stir in. Separate eggs, and beat egg yolks until thick, then stir into cheese mixture. Beat egg whites until stiff and beat in half the sugar, then stir in the remaining sugar. Fold into cheese mixture and put into baking tin. Bake at 350°F (Gas Mark 4) for 1 hour, and leave to cool in the oven. Remove from tin.

Pack in foil *after* freezing, and then in box to avoid crushing.

To serve: Thaw in refrigerator for 8 hours, and eat with fresh or frozen fruit.

Storage time: 1 month.

CHOCOLATE ORANGE MOUSSE

6 oz. plain
  chocolate
½ gill water
½ oz. butter
Juice of 1 small
  orange

3 eggs
¼ pint whipping
  cream
1 tsp caster sugar

Shred chocolate into a small pan, and heat gently with water to a thick cream. Cool slightly and beat in butter. Add egg yolks one at a time, and then orange juice. Whisk egg whites until stiff and fold into chocolate mixture. Put into a serving dish which will go into the freezer. Decorate with piped cream which has been whipped with sugar (if preferred, cream may be piped on when mousse is removed from freezer, just before serving).

Pack serving dish into polythene or foil (if cream topping is used, freeze mousse before packing).

To serve: Thaw in refrigerator for 2 hours.

Storage time: 1 month.

ICEBOX CAKE

6 oz. icing sugar
4 oz. butter
2 medium eggs
2 tsp grated lemon
   rind and 2 tbsp
   lemon juice *or*

2 tbsp cocoa
and 1 tsp coffee
essence *or* 1 tbsp
coffee essence
48 sponge finger
biscuits

Cream butter and sugar until light and fluffy and work in eggs one at a time. Gradually beat in flavourings, and then beat hard until fluffy and smooth. Cover a piece of cardboard with foil and on it place 12 biscuits, curved side down. On this put one-third of the creamed mixture. Put another layer of biscuits in the opposite direction, and more creamed mixture. Repeat layers, ending with biscuits.

Pack by wrapping in foil. This is a large pudding and could be prepared in two portions.

To serve: Unwrap and thaw in refrigerator for 3 hours, then cover completely with whipped cream and serve at once.

Storage time: 1 month.

JUNE

Serious freezing of home-grown fruit and vegetables begins now. Shellfish and salmon are good value. Cream and ice cream will be needed to eat with fresh fruit.

FOOD IN SEASON

Vegetables Asparagus, broad beans, cabbage, carrots, cauliflower, corn-on-the-cob, French beans, globe artichokes, peas, potatoes, spinach, tomatoes.
Fruit Cherries, gooseberries, loganberries, peaches, raspberries, rhubarb, strawberries.
Fish Crab, herring, lobster, plaice, prawns, salmon, shrimps, trout, whitebait.
Meat, Poultry and Game Duckling, guinea fowl.

BULK BUYING CHECKLIST
Cream, ice cream.

NOW IS THE TIME TO FREEZE:

Cabbage, cauliflower, corn-on-the-cob, French beans, globe artichokes, potatoes, cherries, gooseberries, peaches, strawberries

CORN-ON-THE-COB

Corn-on-the-cob can be successfully frozen, but it needs careful cooking afterwards for good results. Leaves and silk threads should be removed from cobs and the cobs graded for size with stems cut short. Cobs for freezing whole should not be starchy and over-ripe, nor have shrunken or under-sized kernels (these cobs may be used for preparing whole kernels for freezing). Blanch small cobs for 4 minutes, medium cobs for 6 minutes and large cobs for 8 minutes. Cool and dry well on absorbent paper. Pack individual ears in freezer paper and freeze immediately in the coldest part of the freezer (individual ears may then be stored for easy handling in quantities in bags). Whole kernels can be scraped from cobs and packaged in containers leaving $\frac{1}{2}$ in. headspace. *Storage time:* 1 year.

There are three ways of cooking frozen corn-on-the-cob:

(*a*) Put frozen unwrapped corn in cold water to cover and put over high heat. Bring to fast boil, then simmer for 5 minutes.

(*b*) Thaw corn completely in packaging, preferably in the refrigerator. Plunge in boiling water and cook 10 minutes.

(*c*) Preheat oven to 350°F (Gas Mark 4) and roast corn for 20 minutes; or wrap in foil and roast on a barbecue, turning frequently.

CABBAGE

It may not be considered worth giving freezer space to cabbage, but if it is popular in the family, spring and summer varieties can be frozen to use until winter supplies are available. Frozen cabbage cannot be used as a salad vegetable while still raw, and must be cooked to be successful. Cabbage should be firm and solid for best results. Wash cabbage very well and shred. Blanch for 1½ minutes and pack in polythene bags. *To serve:* Cook for 8 minutes in boiling water. *Storage time:* 6 months.

CAULIFLOWER

Small firm compact cauliflower heads may be frozen, but it is better to freeze in sprigs. Use heads with close white flowers. Wash them thoroughly and break into sprigs not more than 1 in. across. Add the juice of 1 lemon to the blanching water to keep the cauliflower white. Blanch for 3 minutes, cool and pack in lined boxes. *To serve:* Cook for 10 minutes in boiling water. *Storage time:* 6 months.

FRENCH BEANS

French beans for freezing should be tender and young. Remove any strings from young beans and remove tops and tails. Leave small beans whole, or cut into 1-in. pieces. Blanch whole beans 3 minutes, cut beans 2 minutes. Cool and pack in polythene bags. *To serve:* Cook whole beans for 7 minutes in boiling salted water, cut beans for 5 minutes. *Storage time:* 1 year.

GLOBE ARTICHOKES

Only home-grown globe artichokes should be frozen, as the heads stale quickly. Remove outer leaves from each head and wash artichokes very thoroughly. Trim stalks and remove 'chokes'. Blanch no more than six at a time in 4 quarts boiling water with 1 tbsp lemon juice for 7 minutes. Cool in ice water and drain upside-down on absorbent paper. Pack in plastic or waxed boxes, as polythene will tear. *To serve:* Plunge into boiling water and boil for 5 minutes until leaves are tender and easily removed. Artichoke bottoms may be frozen by removing all green leaves and centre flower, blanching for 5 minutes, then cooling before packing. *Storage time:* 1 year.

POTATOES

Potatoes are best frozen when small and new, but they may also be frozen in cooked form such as chips, croquettes, baked potatoes, creamed potatoes or duchesse potatoes, later in the year. Grade new potatoes for size, scrape and wash. Blanch for 4 minutes, cool and pack in polythene bags. Alternatively, slightly undercook, drain, toss in butter, cool quickly and pack. *To serve:* Cook potatoes in boiling water for 15 minutes. Those which are already cooked can be reheated by plunging the freezing bag into boiling water, removing pan from heat, and leaving for 10 minutes. *Storage time:* 1 year (3 months if fully cooked).

GOOSEBERRIES

It is best to freeze gooseberries in the form in which they will be most conveniently used, i.e. whole and uncooked for jam or pies; purée for making fools. The fruit should be washed in ice-chilled water and dried. For pies the fruit should be frozen when fully ripe in bags or containers without sweetening, and it is a good idea to grade this fruit for size. Smaller, irregularly sized fruit can be frozen for jam-making, and is best frozen slightly under-ripe, in bags, without sweetening. Purée is best made by stewing the fruit in very little water, sieving and sweetening to taste, and packing in cartons with $\frac{1}{2}$ in. headspace. *To serve:* Thaw at room temperature for $2\frac{1}{2}$ hours, or put frozen fruit straight into syrup to cook. *Storage time:* 1 year. The best variety for freezing is *Careless*.

PEACHES

Peaches must be prepared with great care as they discolour quickly. They should be peeled, halved and stoned, then brushed with lemon juice to stop discolouring. Only one peach should be prepared at a time. Peaches may be halved or sliced, and are best packed in 40% syrup (11 oz. sugar to 1 pint water). To prevent browning and softness, it is better, though more troublesome, to peel and stone peaches under cold running water rather than dipping them in boiling water to aid the removal of the skin. Since peaches begin to discolour as soon as they are exposed to the air, it is better to defrost them slowly in a refrigerator and serve while still a little frosty. If they are to be used in cakes or topped with cream, they can be used half-thawed, put into the appropriate dish, and will be ready for eating by the time preparation is finished. *Storage time:* 1 year.

Peaches may also be frozen in the form of a purée to use as a sauce, or for making into ice cream. The peaches should be peeled and stoned, crushed with a silver fork, and mixed with 1 tbsp lemon juice and 4 oz. sugar to each lb of fruit, before packing into containers.

STRAWBERRIES

It is best to freeze strawberries dry without sweetening, as they are then less pulpy on thawing. Hulls should be removed from strawberries which are fully ripe and mature, but firm. The most satisfactory way to freeze strawberries in a sugar or syrup pack is to slice or slightly crush them. Without sweetening, they can be frozen whole, but should be graded for size. For a dry sugar pack, use 4 oz. sugar to each lb of fruit. Use 40% syrup (11 oz. sugar to 1 pint water) if this type of pack is preferred. Ripe strawberries which have been sieved and sweetened to taste may be frozen as purée and make a delicious strawberry ice served in the frozen state. *To serve:* Thaw strawberries at room temperature for $1\frac{1}{2}$ hours. *Storage time:* 1 year. The best varieties for freezing are *Cambridge Vigour, Cambridge Favourite* and *Royal Sovereign*.

CHERRIES

Red cherries are better than black for freezing, but both sweet and sour varieties can be used. The cherries should be firmed in ice-chilled water for 1 hour before freezing, then thoroughly dried. The stones should be removed, as these may flavour fruit during storage. Use glass or plastic containers as the acid in cherry juice tends to remain liquid during freezing, and may leak through cardboard. Cherries for pie-making are best in a dry sugar pack, allowing 8 oz. sugar to 2 lb pitted cherries. For sweet cherries in a syrup pack, 40% syrup (11 oz. sugar to 1 pint water) is best, and for sour cherries 50% or 60% syrup (16 oz. or 25 oz. sugar to 1 pint water) depending on tartness. *To serve:* Thaw at room temperature for 3 hours. *Storage time:* 1 year.

WHEN THERE'S A GLUT, FREEZE:

Gooseberry Sauce, Gooseberry Ice, Strawberry Jam, Strawberry Ice, Strawberry Sauce

GOOSEBERRY SAUCE

1 lb gooseberries	2 tbsp caster sugar
1 oz. butter	

Wash gooseberries, but do not top and tail them. Put in a pan with 2 tbsp water and the butter. Cover and cook 15 minutes on low heat until soft. Put through a sieve and then reheat purée with sugar until dissolved. Chill and pack in small containers. *To serve:* Reheat gently and use with fish, or with steamed puddings. *Storage time:* 3 months.

GOOSEBERRY ICE

1 lb gooseberries   ½ pint double cream
4 oz. caster sugar

Wash gooseberries and put in a pan without topping and tailing. Add 1 tbsp water and sugar and simmer with a lid on for 15 minutes until fruit is soft. Put through a sieve and cool the purée. Whip cream into peaks and fold into the purée, adding a little green colouring if liked. Put into ice tray and freeze for 2 hours. Whisk in a cold basin until smooth and creamy, return to freezer and freeze 1 hour. Pack into storage container and cover. *Storage time:* 3 months.

STRAWBERRY JAM

1½ lb strawberries   4 fl. oz. liquid
2 lb caster sugar   pectin

Mash or sieve strawberries and stir with sugar in a bowl. Leave for 20 minutes, stirring occasionally, then add pectin and stir for 3 minutes. Pack in small waxed or rigid plastic containers, cover tightly and seal. Leave at room temperature for 24–28 hours until jelled before freezing. *To serve:* Thaw at room temperature for 1 hour. *Storage time:* 6 months.

STRAWBERRY ICE

2 lb strawberries	8 oz. sugar
Juice of 1 orange	1 egg white
¼ pint water	

Crush strawberries with orange juice and put through sieve. Put water in pan, stir in sugar and boil for 5 minutes. Cool and stir in strawberries. Freeze to a mush, then put into chilled bowl. Beat well and add stiffly-whipped egg white. Freeze until firm, then pack into storage container, cover and seal. *Storage time:* 1 year.

STRAWBERRY SAUCE

1 lb strawberries	Juice of 2 lemons
6 oz. caster sugar	

Hull and wash fruit, and put through a sieve. Stir in sugar and lemon juice which has been strained, and continue stirring until sugar has dissolved. Pack into waxed or rigid plastic container. *To serve:* Thaw in refrigerator and serve cold over ice cream, cakes or puddings.

PREPARE-AHEAD DISHES

CORNISH PASTIES

1 lb short pastry	1 onion
12 oz. steak	3 tbsp stock
6 oz. potatoes	Salt and pepper

Divide pastry into eight pieces and roll each into a 5-in. circle. Cut steak and potatoes in small dice and chop finely. Season and moisten with stock. Put meat filling in the centre of each circle of pastry, and fold up edges to make half-circles. Seal edges well, giving a fluted appearance, and slightly flatten base of pasties.

Pack in polythene bags; if pasties are baked before freezing, pack in boxes to avoid crushing.

To serve: Unbaked pasties, brush them with egg and bake (without thawing) at 425°F (Gas Mark 7) for 15 minutes, then at 350°F (Gas Mark 4) for 40 minutes. If preferred, pasties may be baked at the same temperature and for the same time before freezing. To serve already-baked pasties, thaw for 12 hours in refrigerator to eat cold, or reheat at 375°F (Gas Mark 5) for 20 minutes.

Storage time: 1 month.

CORNED BEEF ENVELOPES

4 oz. corned beef	1 tsp chopped
1 tbsp tomato	parsley
ketchup	8 oz. short pastry

Mix corned beef, ketchup and parsley. Roll out pastry and cut into 12 squares. Put a spoonful of mixture on each square, and fold into triangles, sealing edges well. Brush with egg or milk. Bake at 425°F (Gas Mark 7) for 15 minutes. Cool.

Pack in foil tray in polythene bag, or in shallow box to avoid crushing.

To serve: Thaw at room temperature for 1 hour to eat cold. These may also be heated if liked.

Storage time: 1 month.

PIZZA

4 oz. plain flour	Oregano or
¼ oz. yeast	marjoram
Salt and pepper	3 oz. cheese
4 medium tomatoes	Olive oil
6 anchovy fillets	

Sift flour with a good pinch of salt and add yeast dissolved in a little tepid water. Blend well and add a little more warm water to make a stiff dough. Knead well, form into a ball, cover with a cloth, and leave in a warm place until double in volume. Roll out to a large disc about ¼ in. thick. Skin and chop tomatoes, and spread on dough, seasoning well with pepper and salt. Arrange anchovy fillets on top and thin slices of cheese, and sprinkle well with herbs and olive oil. Bake at 425°F (Gas Mark 7) for 30 minutes. Cool. Mozzarella cheese should be used, but Bel Paese can be substituted, but should only be added 10 minutes before cooking finishes as it melts quickly. Fresh herbs rather than dried should be used. Anchovies may be omitted from topping as their saltiness may cause rancidity in the fatty cheese during storage, and they can be added at the reheating stage.

Pack in heavy-duty foil.

To serve: Thaw at room temperature for 1 hour, then bake at 375°F (Gas Mark 5) for 25 minutes and serve very hot.

Storage time: 1 month.

PORK WITH ORANGE SAUCE

6 large lean pork chops	½ pint orange juice (fresh, tinned or frozen)
2 medium onions	
2 tbsp vinegar	1 tbsp brown sugar

Toss the meat very lightly in a little seasoned flour and cook in a little oil until browned. Remove from oil and cook sliced onions until just soft. Return chops and onions to pan, pour over orange juice, vinegar and sugar and simmer gently for 30 minutes until chops are cooked through. Cool.

Pack in foil trays, covering with sauce, and with foil lid.

To serve: Heat with lid on at 350°F (Gas Mark 4) for 45 minutes. Garnish with fresh orange slices or segments.

Storage time: 1 month.

SANDWICHES

Sandwiches can be usefully frozen for summer lunch boxes or picnics, and keep well for about 4 weeks, depending on the type of filling. Plain white bread, whole wheat, rye, pumpernickel and fruit breads can be used, together with baps and rolls. Brown bread is good for fish fillings, and fruit bread for cheese or sweet fillings.

Preparation and Packing

Sandwiches are best packed in groups of six or eight rather than individually. An extra slice or crust of bread at each end of the package will prevent drying out, and the sandwiches should be wrapped in heavy-duty foil or polythene bags. If sandwiches are frozen against the freezer wall, this will result in uneven thawing, and it is best to put packages a few inches from the wall of the freezer. Softened fat should be used for spreading sandwich bread, and should be carried right to the edge of the bread to prevent fillings soaking in. Make sure that fillings are well chilled, and fill sandwiches generously. Stack sandwiches and cut with a sharp knife, leaving in large portions (such as half-slices) with crusts on, to prevent drying out. Wrap tightly in Cellophane, then in foil or polythene.

Serving

Thaw in wrappings in refrigerator for 12 hours, or at room temperature for 4 hours. Outer wrappings may be removed for further use, and the inner packet put straight into a lunch box or picnic basket.

Fillings

Avoid certain fillings which do not freeze well. Leave out cooked egg whites which toughen and become dry. Raw vegetables, such as celery, lettuce, tomatoes and carrots should not be used. Salad cream and mayonnaise curdle and separate when frozen and will soak into the bread when thawed. Jam also soaks into the bread during thawing.

GOOSEBERRY PUDDING

4 oz. suet	Pinch of salt
1 oz. butter	1 lb gooseberries
8 oz. self-raising flour	2 oz. sugar

Work together suet, butter, flour and salt, adding a very little water, if needed, to make a dough. Roll out, and line 1-lb foil basin with dough. Top and tail the gooseberries, fill the basin, and add sugar. Cover with crust and pinch the edges together. Cover with a cloth, and boil for 2½ hours. Cool in basin.

Pack by covering basin with lid of heavy-duty foil.

To serve: Steam for 1 hour, turn out and serve with cream or custard.

Storage time: 2 months.

GOOSEBERRY SORBET

2 lb green goose-
    berries
6 oz. caster sugar
1½ pints water
Juice of 1 lemon

Green vegetable
    colouring
2 fl. oz. Maraschino
2 fl. oz. white rum

Cook gooseberries with sugar and water, add lemon juice and a little green colouring and put through a sieve. Cool and freeze to a thick batter. Add Maraschino and rum, and continue freezing. This ice will not become solid.

Pack in waxed or rigid plastic containers.

To serve: Scoop into glasses.

Storage time: 2 months.

VIENNESE RED CURRANT ICE

1 lb red currants
4 oz. red currant
    jelly
1 pint water
1 large ripe tomato
4 oz. raspberries
Juice and rind of ½
    lemon

3 oz. caster sugar
Red vegetable
    colouring
4 egg yolks
2 fl. oz. white rum
    or brandy
½ pint double cream

Remove currants from stalks and simmer with red currant jelly, hot water, tomato, raspberries, juice and rind of lemon, sugar and colouring until the fruit is a pulp. Cool and add well-beaten egg yolks and rum or brandy. Rub through a sieve, and freeze to a batter. Add whipped cream and continue freezing for 2 hours.

Pack into waxed or rigid plastic containers.

To serve: Scoop into glasses.

Storage time: 2 months.

TEA ICE

2 oz. tea
1 pint water
3 eggs

½ tsp vanilla essence
3 oz. caster sugar
½ pint double cream

Warm a teapot, put in the tea and pour on boiling water. Leave to infuse for 5 minutes, strain and leave until completely cold. Beat the whole eggs with the sugar and vanilla essence for about 5 minutes, until white and thick. Add the cold tea by degrees, whipping all the time. Fold in thickly whipped cream and freeze for 2 hours, stirring once during freezing.

Pack in waxed or rigid plastic container.

To serve: Scoop out and serve with small sweet biscuits.

Storage time: 2 months.

COFFEE ICE

4 heaped tbsp
  freshly ground
  coffee

1 pint water
3 oz. caster sugar
½ pint single cream

Put coffee into a hot dry coffee pot, pour on boiling · water, and leave to stand for 10 minutes. Strain and mix with sugar. Cool and mix with cream. Freeze for 45 minutes, stir and continue freezing for 1½ hours.

Pack in waxed or rigid plastic containers.

To serve: Pile into small cups and serve with sweet biscuits

Storage time: 2 months.

JULY

This is the month of maximum preservation of garden produce, and bargains at the greengrocer's. It is also a good month for fish and shellfish. Many cooked dishes are needed for the beginning of the school holidays and for picnics.

FOOD IN SEASON

Vegetables Asparagus, aubergines, broad beans, cabbage, carrots, cauliflower, corn-on-the-cob, courgettes, French beans, globe artichokes, herbs, peas, peppers, potatoes, spinach, tomatoes.
Fruit Apricots, blackcurrants, cherries, figs, gooseberries, loganberries, melons, nectarines, peaches, plums, raspberries, red currants, strawberries.
Fish Crab, haddock, halibut, lobster, plaice, prawns, red mullet, salmon, salmon trout, shrimps, sole, trout.

WHAT TO BUY FROM THE SHOPS
Bread (including baps and rolls), fruit bread.

BULK BUYING CHECKLIST
Fish fingers, beefburgers, chips, peas, ice cream, pasties, sausage rolls, cream.

NOW IS THE TIME TO FREEZE:

Aubergines, courgettes, herbs, peppers,
apricots, blackcurrants, figs, loganberries,
melons, nectarines, raspberries, red currants

AUBERGINES

Aubergines for freezing should be medium-sized and mature, with tender seeds, or the results may be rubbery in texture. The aubergines should be peeled and cut into 1-in. slices, blanched for 4 minutes, then chilled and dried on absorbent paper. The slices should be packed in cartons, with the layers separated by Cellophane. *To serve:* Cook in boiling water for 5 minutes. *Storage time:* 1 year. Aubergines may also be cooked before freezing, but should then only be stored for 1 month. The peeled slices should be coated in thin batter, or egg and breadcrumbs, then fried in deep fat, well-drained and cooled, and packed in cartons in layers separated by Cellophane. For serving, they can be heated in a slow oven, or part-thawed and deep-fried.

COURGETTES

Do not peel courgettes, but cut in $\frac{1}{2}$-in. slices and blanch for 3 minutes before packing in cartons or polythene bags. *To serve:* Fry courgettes in oil with plenty of salt and pepper. *Storage time:* 6 months.

HERBS

It is not a good idea to freeze herbs for garnishing, since they become limp on thawing. Their flavour is useful for sauces, soups, sandwich fillings and butters, and their colour remains good in the freezer. Parsley, mint, chives, fennel, basil and thyme are useful herbs to freeze, and they can be prepared in two ways:

(a) Pick sprigs of herbs, wash, drain and dry well. Pack whole in polythene bags. These can be crumbled while still frozen to add to dishes, but the leaves tend to be a bit leathery and difficult to rub into small pieces.

(b) Wash herbs well and remove from stems. Cut finely and pack into ice-cube trays, adding a little water. Freeze until solid, then wrap each cube in foil, and package quantities in polythene bags, labelling carefully. A cube can be put into casseroles or sauces while still frozen and just before serving time.

PEPPERS

Green and red peppers can be frozen separately or in mixed packages. They may be frozen in halves for stuffing and baking, or sliced for use in stews and sauces. Wash firm crisp peppers carefully, cut off stems and caps and remove seeds and membranes. Blanch halves for 3 minutes and slices for 2 minutes. Pack in polythene bags or in rigid containers. *To serve:* Thaw before using, allowing 1½ hours at room temperature. *Storage time:* 1 year.

Roast red peppers may also be frozen and are

very useful. Put peppers under a hot grill until charred, then plunge in cold water and rub off skins. Remove caps and seeds and pack tightly in rigid containers. covering with brine solution (1 tbsp salt to 1 pint water), leaving 1 in. headspace, and cover. *To serve:* Let the peppers thaw in containers and serve in a little of the brine solution to which has been added 1 tbsp olive oil, a crushed clove of garlic and a shake of black pepper. They may also be served as an appetizer sliced with anchovies, onion rings and capers and dressed in olive oil and basil.

APRICOTS

Apricot halves can be frozen without peeling, but the skins may toughen in the freezer, and unpeeled halves can be dropped into boiling water for $\frac{1}{2}$ minute to prevent this. Peeled slices can be used fresh or cooked after freezing. Apricots discolour quickly, and should only be prepared in small quantities. Very ripe fruit is best frozen as purée or sauce. *To freeze apricot halves:* Wash them under cold running water, cut into halves and take out stones. Drop into boiling water for $\frac{1}{2}$ minute. Chill in iced water and drain. Pack in dry sugar, using 4 oz. sugar to each lb of fruit, or use 40% syrup (11 oz. sugar to 1 pint water). *To freeze apricot slices:* Peel fruit quickly, then slice directly into container quarter-full of 40% syrup (11 oz. sugar to 1 pint water). Top up with syrup to keep fruit covered, put Cellophane on top, and allow $\frac{1}{2}$ in. headspace. *To serve:* Thaw $3\frac{1}{2}$ hours at room temperature, and use as soon as thawed or apricots will go brown. *Storage time:* 1 year.

BLACKCURRANTS

Blackcurrants should be washed in ice-chilled water, then dried gently. For later use in jam-making, pack dry into polythene bags. For a dry sugar pack, use 8 oz. sugar to 1 lb prepared berries, mixing until most of the sugar is dissolved, and pack in bags or cartons. If a syrup pack is preferred, use 40% syrup (11 oz. sugar to 1 pint water). Blackcurrants are excellent frozen in the form of a syrup or purée to use for drinks, puddings and ices, or to serve as a sauce. *To serve:* Thaw at room temperature for 45 minutes. *Storage time:* 1 year. The best varieties to grow for freezing are *Boskoop Giant* and *Wellington*.

FIGS

Fresh green and purple figs can be frozen. They should be fully ripe, soft and sweet, with small seeds and slightly shrivelled but unsplit skins. Wash figs in chilled water, removing stems with a sharp knife, and handling carefully to avoid bruising. Pack whole and peeled, or unpeeled in polythene bags, without sweetening; or pack peeled figs in 30% syrup (7 oz. sugar to 1 pint water). *To serve:* Thaw at room temperature for $1\frac{1}{2}$ hours. Unsweetened figs may be eaten raw or cooked in syrup. *Storage time:* 1 year.

LOGANBERRIES

Use fully ripe berries, but if they are at all 'woody', prepare them as a purée for freezing. Wash small quantities of loganberries in ice-chilled water and drain almost dry in absorbent paper. Pack dry and unsweetened in polythene bags or in boxes, or in dry sugar,

oz. sugar to 2 lb fruit. If a syrup
referred, use 50% syrup (16 oz. sugar
pint water). Crushed berries can be
and sweetened, allowing 4 oz. sugar to
1 pint of crushed berries, stirred until dissolved, and packed leaving ½ in. headspace.
To serve: Thaw at room temperature for 3
hours. *Storage time:* 1 year.

MELONS

All varieties of melon can be frozen, though
watermelon is a little difficult to prepare because of the seeds distributed through the
flesh. Cut melon flesh in cubes or balls and
toss in lemon juice before packing in 30%
syrup (7 oz. sugar to 1 pint water). *To serve:*
Defrost unopened in the refrigerator and eat
while a little frosty, without allowing melon
to thaw completely. *Storage time:* 1 year.

NECTARINES

Nectarines must be prepared with great care
as they discolour quickly. They should be
peeled, halved and stoned, then brushed with
lemon juice to stop browning, and only a few
fruit should be prepared at a time. Nectarines
may be halved or sliced, and packed in 40%
syrup (11 oz. sugar to 1 pint water). It is usual
to dip nectarines in boiling water to remove
skins, but for freezing it is better to peel and
stone them under cold water to prevent
softness and browning. They begin to discolour as soon as exposed to the air both before
and after freezing. *To serve:* Thaw slowly in
container in the refrigerator for about 3 hours,
and use while still a little frosty. *Storage
time:* 1 year.

94

RASPBERRIES

Raspberries freeze very well, their colour and flavour remaining almost unchanged after storage. If frozen without sugar, their texture also remains like that of fresh fruit. Fruit should be picked over carefully, discarding any hard or seedy berries. Wash fruit in ice-chilled water and dry very thoroughly. Freeze without sugar in cartons or polythene bags. Raspberries may also be frozen in sugar, allowing 4 oz. sugar to 1 lb fruit, or can be packed in 30% syrup (7 oz. sugar to 1 pint water). *To serve:* Thaw at room temperature for 3 hours. *Storage time:* 1 year. Raspberries may also be frozen as purée, which makes a useful base for sauce, fruit drinks and milk shakes, and mousses. The berries should be put through a sieve and sweetened with 4 oz. sugar to 1 pint purée. When the sugar has dissolved, pack the purée in containers, or in small quantities in ice-cube trays. When frozen, each cube should be wrapped in foil and packed in bulk in a polythene bag. A single cube will be enough for one serving.

RED CURRANTS

Redcurrants should be stripped from the stem with a fork and washed in ice-chilled water, then dried gently. For a dry sugar pack, use 8 oz. sugar to 1 lb prepared berries, mixing until most of the sugar is dissolved. If a syrup pack is preferred, use 40% syrup (11 oz. sugar to 1 pint water). Redcurrants can also be cooked in a little water and sieved, and the purée sweetened with 6 oz. sugar to 1 pint purée. This purée is very good to use as a sauce for a steamed pudding, a mousse, or for serving with raspberries. *To serve:* Thaw red-currants at room temperature for 45 minutes. *Storage time:* 1 year.

WHEN THERE'S A GLUT, FREEZE:

Fresh Fruit Ice, Fresh Fruit Mousse,
Fresh Fruit Whip, Fresh Fruit Cream,
Raspberry Sauce, Raspberry Jam,
Fruit Pie Fillings, Soft Fruit Syrups

FRESH FRUIT ICE

½ pint fruit purée   ¾ pint cream
1½ tbsp caster sugar

Stir together fruit purée and sugar, and fold into lightly whipped cream. Freeze without stirring. Pack into storage containers, cover and seal. This is very good made with fresh raspberries, or with apricots poached in a little vanilla-flavoured syrup before sieving. *Storage time:* 3 months.

FRESH FRUIT MOUSSE

¼ pint fruit purée   2 egg whites
1 oz. caster sugar   Juice of ½ lemon
¼ pint double cream

Mix fruit purée and sugar. Whip cream lightly, and whip egg whites stiffly. Add lemon juice to fruit, then fold in cream and egg whites. A little colouring may be added if the fruit is pale. Pack in serving dish covered with foil. *To serve:* Thaw in refrigerator without lid for 2 hours. *Storage time:* 1 month.

FRESH FRUIT WHIP

1 lb rhubarb, Sugar
 gooseberries or ½ pint evaporated
 blackcurrants   milk

Prepare fruit and stew in very little water with sugar to taste until tender. Put through a sieve and fold into whipped evaporated milk. Pack in individual dishes and cover with foil. *To serve:* Thaw at room temperature for 2 hours. *Storage time:* 2 months.

FRESH FRUIT CREAM

1 lb raspberries, ¾ pint water
 currants or goose- 6 oz. sugar
 berries   2 tbsp cornflour

Clean fruit. Bring water to boil, add fruit and sugar, and boil until fruit is soft. Mix cornflour with a little cold water, blend into hot liquid, and bring back to boil. Cool and pack in serving dish covered with foil. *To serve:* Thaw in refrigerator for 1 hour and serve with cream. *Storage time:* 1 month.

RASPBERRY SAUCE

Raspberries   Sugar

Put raspberries in pan with very little water and heat very slowly until juice runs. Put through a sieve and sweeten to taste. Pack into small waxed or rigid plastic containers. *To serve:* Thaw in container in refrigerator for 2 hours. Serve with puddings or ice cream. *Storage time:* 1 year.

RASPBERRY JAM

1½ lb raspberries   4 fl. oz. liquid pectin
3 lb caster sugar

Mash or sieve raspberries and stir with sugar.
Leave for 20 minutes, stirring occasionally,
then add pectin and stir for 3 minutes. Pack
in small waxed or rigid plastic containers,
cover tightly and seal. Leave at room temperature for 24–28 hours until jelled before
freezing. *To serve:* Thaw at room temperature
for 1 hour. *Storage time:* 1 year.

FRUIT PIE FILLINGS

1½ lb fruit   2 tbsp tapioca
1 tbsp lemon juice   flakes
8 oz. sugar   Pinch of salt

Mix all ingredients well in a bowl and leave to
stand for 15 minutes. Line a pie plate with
foil, leaving 6-in. rim. Put filling into foil, fold
over and freeze. Remove frozen fillings from
pie plate, pack and freeze. Good combinations
of fruit are raspberry and apple, rhubarb and
orange, apricot and pineapple. Single fruits such
as cherries and blackberries may be prepared
in the same way. Pack in foil or polythene.
To serve: Line pie plate with pastry, put in
frozen filling, dot with butter, cover with pastry
lid, make slits in top crust, and bake at 425°F
(Gas Mark 7) for 45 minutes. *Storage time:*
1 year.

SOFT FRUIT SYRUPS

Raspberries,	Sugar
blackcurrants,	
strawberries,	
redcurrants	

Fruit may be used singly, or combined, e.g.
raspberries and redcurrants. Use fresh clean
ripe fruit and avoid washing if possible,
discarding mouldy or damaged fruit. Add $\frac{1}{4}$
pint water for each lb of raspberries or strawberries; $\frac{1}{2}$ pint for each lb of currants. Cook
very gently (this can be done in the oven in
a covered jar) for about 1 hour, crushing fruit
at intervals. Turn into jelly bag or clean cloth,
and leave to drip overnight. Measure cold juice,
and add $\frac{3}{4}$ lb sugar to each pint of juice. Stir
well until dissolved. Pack into small waxed or
rigid plastic containers, leaving $\frac{1}{2}$ in. headspace. Syrup can also be poured into ice-cube
trays, and each cube wrapped in foil after
freezing. *To serve:* Thaw at room temperature
for 1 hour, and use for sauces, mousses and
drinks. *Storage time:* 1 year.

PREPARE-AHEAD DISHES

GREEN PEA SOUP

2 lb green peas	Mixed herbs
1 oz. butter	3 pints stock
1 small onion	Salt and pepper
1 small lettuce	

Put peas, butter, grated onion, shredded lettuce, and a small bunch of herbs in a pan with a tight-fitting lid. Cook slowly for 10 minutes. Add stock, salt and pepper, and simmer for 1½ hours. Put through a sieve and cool.

Pack in waxed or rigid plastic containers, leaving headspace.

To serve: Reheat gently, adjusting seasoning to taste, and stir in ½ gill cream just before serving. Fried or toasted croutons, or small pieces of crisp bacon are good garnishes for this soup.

Storage time: 2 months.

RATATOUILLE

2 large onions	4 large ripe tomatoes
2 green or red peppers	2 cloves garlic
2 large aubergines	¼ pint olive oil
3 courgettes	Salt and pepper

Cut peppers in thin strips, removing cores and seeds, and slice onions thinly. Slice unpeeled aubergines and courgettes thinly, sprinkle with salt and leave in a colander for 1 hour. Drain and dry well. Heat oil in a heavy pan and cook onions gently for 10 minutes. Add peppers, aubergines and courgettes and continue simmering for 30 minutes with lid on pan. Add chopped tomatoes, crushed garlic and seasoning and simmer for 45 minutes. Leave to cool and remove excess oil.

Pack in waxed or rigid plastic containers.

To serve: Thaw in refrigerator for 5 hours, and use as first course, or as an accompaniment to meat or fish. The dish is good sprinkled with chopped parsley and served with hot French bread.

Storage time: 1 month.

STUFFED GREEN PEPPERS

4 large green peppers	1 tsp marjoram or thyme
8 oz. Patna rice	1 tbsp lemon juice
2 tbsp chopped parsley	2 tbsp olive oil
	Salt and pepper

Cut peppers in half lengthways, remove seeds and membrane, and rinse 'shells' thoroughly. Cook rice in boiling water until just tender, drain and rinse well. Mix with parsley, marjoram or thyme, lemon juice, half the oil, salt and pepper. Fill peppers with this mixture. Pour remaining oil into a shallow baking dish, put in peppers and cover with foil. Bake at 325°F (Gas Mark 3) for 1 hour, adding a little more oil if necessary. Cool completely. A little cooked minced meat may be added to the filling.

Pack in waxed containers.

To serve: Put peppers in an oiled dish, cover with foil, and heat at 350°F (Gas Mark 4) for 30 minutes. Home-made tomato sauce is good if poured over the peppers and heated through.

Storage time: 2 months.

SHRIMP BISQUE

2 sticks celery	Salt and pepper
4 oz. mushrooms	Bay leaf
1 small onion	Pinch of nutmeg
1 carrot	2 tbsp lemon juice
2 oz. butter	2 tbsp white wine
2 pints chicken stock	6 oz. shrimps

Cut celery, mushrooms, onion and carrot in small pieces and cook gently in butter for 10 minutes. Add stock, seasoning, bay leaf, nutmeg and lemon juice, and simmer for 20 minutes. Put through a sieve. Add wine and shrimps and simmer for 5 minutes. Cool and remove fat.

Pack into containers, leaving headspace.

To serve: Reheat in a double boiler, stirring gently. When thawed, stir in ½ pint double cream and continue reheating without boiling.

Storage time: 1 month.

POTTED SHRIMPS

Shrimps	Ground mace and
Butter	cloves
Salt and pepper	

Cook freshly caught shrimps, cool in cooking liquid and shell. Pack tightly into waxed cartons. Melt butter, season with salt, pepper and a little mace and cloves. Cool butter and pour over shrimps. Chill until cold.

Pack by covering with lids and sealing with freezer tape.

To serve: Thaw in containers at room temperature for 2 hours, or heat in double boiler until butter has melted and shrimps are warm to serve on toast.

Storage time: 6 months.

PICNIC PIES

8 oz. pie veal	Salt and pepper
2 oz. mushrooms	1 oz. butter
2 oz. lean bacon	¾ pint stock
1 oz. plain flour	12 oz. short pastry

Mince or chop veal and bacon. Mix flour with salt and pepper, and roll the meat in this mixture. Melt butter and fry meat until golden brown. Add sliced mushrooms and stock, bring to boil and simmer for 1 hour. Cool completely. Line 12 deep patty tins with pastry, put in cold filling, and cover with pastry lids. Brush with beaten egg and bake at 400°F (Gas Mark 6) for 25 minutes. Cool.

Pack in foil trays and polythene bags.

To serve: Thaw at room temperature for 2 hours (or pack in picnic basket for 2 hours).

Storage time: 2 months.

CHERRY ALMOND TART

8 oz. short pastry	4 oz. ground almonds
8 oz. stoned cooking cherries	6 oz. icing sugar
	2 eggs

Line a pie plate or foil dish with pastry and prick the pastry well. Fill with cherries. Mix ground almonds, sugar and eggs one at a time to make a soft paste. Pour over cherries and bake at 400°F (Gas Mark 6) for 25 minutes. Cool.

Pack in polythene bag or heavy-duty foil.

To serve: Thaw in wrappings at room temperature for 3 hours.

Storage time: 2 months.

BLACKCURRANT FLAN

8 oz. plain flour	1 small egg
1 tsp cinnamon	1½ tsp lemon juice
5 oz. butter	1½ lb fresh black-
1½ oz. ground	currants
almonds	6 oz. sugar
1½ oz. caster sugar	

Mix flour and cinnamon and work in butter until mixture is like fine breadcrumbs. Mix in almonds and caster sugar and make into a paste with the egg and lemon juice. Divide mixture to make two flans and line flan rings or foil cases, reserving some pastry for decoration (this pastry is very delicate to handle). Put half the prepared fruit in each flan case and sprinkle evenly with sugar. Cover flans with pastry lattice. The flans may be frozen uncooked or cooked, and are less likely to be soggy if frozen before baking.

Pack in foil, or put foil cases into polythene bags.

To serve: Brush lattice of unbaked flan with water, sprinkle with caster sugar and put in cold oven set at 400°F (Gas Mark 6) and bake for 45 minutes. The flan may be baked before freezing at 400°F (Gas Mark 6) for 30 minutes, then thawed in loose wrappings at room temperature for 3 hours.

Storage time: 2 months.

PEACHES IN WHITE WINE

8 peaches	8 oz. sugar
½ pint white wine	1 tbsp Kirsch

Peel peaches and cut in halves. Put into oven dish, cut sides down, cover with wine and sprinkle with sugar. Bake at 375°F (Gas Mark 5) for 40 minutes. Stir in Kirsch and cool.

Pack in leak-proof containers, allowing two peach halves to each container, and covering with syrup.

To serve: Heat at 350°F (Gas Mark 4) for 45 minutes, adding a little more Kirsch if liked, and serve with cream.

Storage time: 2 months.

BAKED FRESH APRICOTS

2 lb fresh apricots	Juice of 1½ lemons
6 oz. caster sugar	

Cut fruit in half and remove stones. Put into covered ovenware dish with sugar and lemon juice. Bake at 300°F (Gas Mark 2) for 1 hour. Cool.

Pack in waxed or rigid plastic containers.

To serve: Thaw in refrigerator for 3 hours and serve with cream.

Storage time: 1 year.

RASPBERRY PUDDING

1 lb raspberries	4 oz. fresh white
4 oz. caster sugar	breadcrumbs
1 oz. butter	3 eggs

Heat raspberries gently with sugar until the juice runs. Put through a sieve, reheat gently and add butter. Pour over breadcrumbs and leave for 30 minutes. Add beaten eggs and mix well and put into 2-pint oven dish. Bake at 350°F (Gas Mark 4) for 1 hour. Cool.

Pack by wrapping dish in foil, or turn out pudding when cold and wrap in foil.

To serve: Thaw at room temperature for 3 hours, dust with icing sugar and serve with cream.

SUMMER FRUIT BOWL

1 lb gooseberries	4 oz. raspberries
4 oz. redcurrants	¼ pint water
4 oz. blackcurrants	6 oz. caster sugar

Top and tail gooseberries and remove currants from stalks. Put in water with sugar and bring slowly to the boil. Simmer very gently for 5 minutes without breaking the fruit. Cool and stir in raspberries.

Pack in waxed or rigid plastic containers.

To serve: Thaw in refrigerator for 3 hours, and serve with cream.

Storage time: 1 year.

PICNIC TEA LOAF

1 lb mixed dried fruit	1 egg
8 oz. sugar	2 tbsp marmalade
½ pint warm tea	1 lb self-raising flour

Soak fruit with sugar and tea overnight. Stir egg and marmalade into fruit and mix well with flour. Pour into two 1-lb loaf tins and bake at 325°F (Gas Mark 3) for 1¾ hours. Cool in tins for 15 minutes before turning out. Cool.

Pack in polythene bags or foil.

To serve: Thaw in wrappings for 3 hours, slice and butter.

Storage time: 4 months.

AUGUST

The summer vegetables are coming to an end, but plenty of autumn fruit and vegetables are available. The shooting season begins, with grouse and hare, both excellent when frozen as raw materials or as cooked dishes. There will also be a demand for picnic and holiday food prepared in advance.

FOOD IN SEASON

Vegetables Aubergines, cabbage, cauliflower, corn-on-the-cob, French beans, globe artichokes, peas, peppers, runner beans, spinach, tomatoes.
Fruit Apples, blackberries, damsons, figs, melons, peaches, pears, plums.
Fish Crab, haddock, halibut, lobster, plaice, prawns, salmon, sole, trout, turbot.
Meat, Poultry and Game Grouse, hare.

NOW IS THE TIME TO FREEZE:

Runner beans, tomatoes, apples, blackberries, damsons, pears, plums, grouse, hare

RUNNER BEANS

It is important that runner beans should not be shredded finely for freezing, or the cooked result may be pulpy and tasteless. Only tender young beans without strings should be frozen. The beans should be cut in pieces, and blanched for 2 minutes. After cooling, pack in polythene bags. *To serve:* Cook in boiling water for 7 minutes. *Storage time:* 1 year.

TOMATOES

Frozen tomatoes cannot be used for salads, since they become slushy on thawing. Their flavour and colour remain good, and they can be frozen whole for later cooking, and preserved in various other forms. To freeze whole tomatoes, choose small ripe fruit, wipe clean and remove stems. Pack in usable quantities (8 oz. or 1 lb) in polythene bags. *To serve:* Thaw at room temperature for 2 hours before cooking. When they have thawed, the skins will slip off easily, and can be removed before a dish is made. Frozen tomatoes can be added directly to a soup or stew, but it will then be necessary to remove skins after cooking. *Storage time:* 1 month. Tomato pulp is also useful to store in the freezer. Prepare the tomatoes by putting them into boiling water until the skins crack, then removing the skins and cores and simmering the tomatoes in their own juice for 5 minutes until soft. Put through a sieve, cool and pack in cartons. *Storage time:* 1 year.

APPLES

Apples for freezing should be crisp and firm, particularly when they are packaged as pie slices. Those which tend to burst and become fluffy in cooking can be frozen as purée. To freeze apples for pies and puddings, choose firm crisp apples. Peel and core, and drop apples into cold water. Slice medium-sized apples into twelfths, large ones into sixteenths. Apples are best packed with sugar, using a proportion of 8 oz. sugar to 2 lb fruit. For a syrup pack, use 40% syrup (11 oz. sugar to 1 pint water), quarter-filling pack with syrup and slicing apples into containers, finishing with more syrup if necessary, covering with Cellophane, and leaving ½ in. headspace. Apple purée should be made with the minimum of water, and should be sweetened with 4 oz. sugar to 1 pint pulp. *To serve:* Thaw apples in container in refrigerator for 3 hours and use quickly to avoid discoloration. *Storage time:* 1 month.

PEARS

Pears do not freeze very well, owing to their delicate flavour, and the fact that their flesh does not keep its paleness. They are useful to keep in small quantities, however, to add variety of flavour and colour to winter fruit salads. Ripe, but not over-ripe, pears with a strong flavour, should be used. Peel and quarter them, remove cores and dip pieces in lemon juice immediately. Poach pears in 30% syrup (7 oz. sugar to 1 pint water) for 1½ minutes. Drain and cool, and pack in cold 30% syrup. A little vanilla sugar, or a vanilla pod poached in the syrup, will improve the flavour. *To serve:* Thaw in covered container for 3 hours at room temperature. *Storage time:* 1 year.

BLACKBERRIES

Use fully ripe blackberries that are dark and glossy, and avoid any with woody pips or with green patches. Wash the berries in small quantities in ice-chilled water and drain almost dry in absorbent paper. Pack dry and unsweetened, or in dry sugar, allowing 8 oz. sugar to 2 lb fruit. If a syrup pack is preferred, use 50% syrup (16 oz. sugar to 1 pint water) and allow headspace. Crushed berries can be sieved and sweetened, allowing 4 oz. sugar to 1 pint of crushed berries, stirred until dissolved, and packed into cartons, leaving $\frac{1}{2}$ in. headspace. *To serve:* Thaw at room temperature for 3 hours. *Storage time:* 1 year.

PLUMS

The skins of plums tend to toughen during storage, and the stones flavour the fruit, so an unsweetened dry pack is not recommended. If preparation time is short, however, it is possible to pack plums raw in polythene bags to freeze. They can be cooked in syrup on removal from the freezer, but tend to darken quickly and become slushy, so should be eaten quickly. Plums are best prepared by cutting in half, removing stones, and packing in 40% syrup (11 oz. sugar to 1 pint water) in waxed or rigid plastic containers. They may also be packed in dry sugar in layers in rigid containers, and will be good to eat without further treatment, but should be eaten up quickly because they darken on thawing. Plums may also be cooked completely and frozen, but this may involve leaving in stones which will flavour the fruit. *To serve:* Thaw at room temperature for 2½ hours. *Storage time:* 1 year.

DAMSONS

The skins of damsons become tough during freezing, and the stones flavour the fruit, so it is better to freeze them as purée. If they are to be frozen whole, wash the fruit in ice-chilled water, cut in half and remove stones, and pack in 50% syrup (16 oz. sugar to 1 pint water). Damsons may also be cooked in syrup for freezing, but it is more difficult to remove the stones. If purée is preferred, cook damsons in a little water, sieve, and sweeten in a proportion of 6 oz. sugar to 1 pint purée. *To serve:* Thaw at room temperature for 2½ hours. *Storage time:* 1 year.

GROUSE

Grouse should be plucked and drawn before freezing, and prepared for cooking, after hanging to individual taste. If birds are old, they are best frozen in the form of a casserole or pie. Young birds should be packed in polythene bags, with all air excluded, and with padding over any protruding bones. *To serve:* Thaw in wrappings in the refrigerator, allowing 5 hours per lb. Start cooking as soon as game is thawed and still cold to prevent loss of juices. *Storage time:* 6–8 months.

HARE

If plenty of hares are available, it is a good idea to freeze some as pâté, pie, or Jugged Hare to be used within a month or two, and to freeze raw joints for later use. A hare should be hung head downwards, with a cup to catch the blood. It can be hung for up to 5 days before freezing, but this must be in a cool place. Skin and clean the hare, wiping the cavity well with a damp cloth. A hare may be frozen whole for roasting, but is more conveniently cut into joints. Each piece should be wrapped in Cellophane, excluding air, then the joints packed together in polythene; one or two pieces can then be extracted for a small recipe. Blood may be frozen separately in a carton. *To serve:* Thaw in wrappings in refrigerator overnight. *Storage time:* 6–8 months.

WHEN THERE'S A GLUT, FREEZE:

Tomato Juice, Tomato Sauce

TOMATO JUICE

Use ripe tomatoes, core and quarter them, and simmer them with a lid on, but add no liquid, for 10 minutes. Put through muslin, cool and pack into cartons, leaving 1 in. headspace. *To serve:* Thaw juice for 1 hour in container in the refrigerator, and season with salt, pepper and a squeeze of lemon juice. *Storage time:* 1 year.

TOMATO SAUCE

1 oz. butter
1 small sliced onion
1 small sliced carrot
1 oz. chopped ham
1 lb sliced tomatoes

1 pint stock
Thyme, parsley and
  bay leaf
½ oz. cornflour

Melt butter and fry onion and carrot until golden. Add tomatoes, ham, stock and herbs, and simmer for 30 minutes. Sieve, thicken with cornflour and season lightly with salt and pepper. Cook for 5 minutes, stirring well. Cool, put into small containers and seal. *To serve:* Thaw in top of double boiler, stirring well, and adjusting seasoning. *Storage time:* 1 year.

TOMATO SOUP

2 lb tomatoes	2 oz. butter
2 oz. mushrooms	3 pints stock
2 medium onions	2 oz. rice flour
1 leek	2 egg yolks
2 sticks celery	¼ pint creamy milk
Juice of 1 lemon	Pinch of sugar
Parsley, thyme and	Salt and pepper
bay leaf	Red colouring

Cut tomatoes in slices. Slice mushrooms, onions, leek and celery and cook lightly in butter. Add the lemon juice, herbs and stock and tomatoes and simmer for 30 minutes. Sieve the mixture. In a bowl, mix egg yolks, rice flour and milk until creamy and add a little of the hot tomato mixture, stirring gently. Add remaining liquid and cook very gently for 10 minutes without boiling. Season to taste with salt and pepper and sugar, and colour if necessary.

Pack after cooling into cartons, leaving headspace.

To serve: Reheat in a double boiler, stirring gently.

Storage time: 2 months.

CHICKEN CACCIATORE

8 chicken joints	1 lb ripe tomatoes
4 tbsp olive oil	Flour, salt and
1 large onion	pepper
2 green peppers	

Chop the onion and cook in oil until soft and golden, but not brown. Remove from oil and keep hot. Mix flour with salt and pepper and toss chicken pieces in this. Fry in oil until golden. Add chopped peppers and tomatoes, cover and simmer for 15 minutes. Add a little chicken stock if dish is becoming a little dry. Cover again and simmer for 45 minutes. Cool and skim off excess oil.

Pack in waxed or rigid plastic containers, or in foil trays with lids, making sure sauce covers chicken pieces.

To serve: Heat at 350°F (Gas Mark 4) for 45 minutes.

Storage time: 1 month.

CREAMED CHICKEN

1 boiling chicken	Parsley and bay leaf
1 small onion	Salt, pepper and
1 clove	nutmeg
1½ pints milk	1 tbsp cornflour

Put chicken into a deep casserole, and pour in milk, together with the onion stuck with clove, herbs and seasonings. Cover and cook at 300°F (Gas Mark 2) for 3 hours. Remove chicken and cut in thin slices. Strain milk and thicken with cornflour, adjusting seasoning. Mix chicken and sauce and cool.

Pack in waxed or rigid plastic containers, or in foil trays with lids.

To serve: Reheat in a double boiler.

Storage time: 1 month.

STUFFED MARROW

1 medium marrow	1 medium onion
1 lb cooked beef or lamb	½ pint stock
6 oz. fresh white breadcrumbs	Salt and pepper

Cut marrow into 2-in. slices, removing seeds and pith, and cook in boiling water for 3 minutes. Drain well and arrange in foil container or greased oven dish. Mince the meat and mix with breadcrumbs, the onion which has been chopped and softened in a little fat, stock and seasonings. A little tomato purée may be added for flavouring, and the stock may be thickened with a little cornflour if a firmer mixture is liked. Cook the mixture for 10 minutes, then fill the marrow rings.

Pack by covering dish with lid of heavy-duty foil.

To serve: Reheat at 375°F (Gas Mark 5) for 1¼ hours, removing lid for final 15 minutes.

Storage time: 1 month.

BACON PASTIES

12 oz. short pastry	1 large onion
8 oz. minced raw steak	Salt and pepper
6 oz. streaky bacon	½ tsp Worcestershire sauce
4 oz. lamb's kidney	

Roll out six 7-in. pastry rounds. Chop all ingredients finely and mix well together. Put a spoonful of mixture on each pastry round and form into pasty shapes, sealing edges well. Place on wetted baking sheet and bake at 425°F (Gas Mark 7) for 45 minutes. Cool.

Pack in foil tray in polythene bag, or in individual polythene bags.

To serve: Thaw 2 hours at room temperature.

Storage time: 1 month.

SAUSAGE AND ONION PIE

8 oz. short pastry	1 onion
8 oz. pork sausage	1 egg
meat	1 tsp mixed herbs

Line foil pie plate with pastry. Mix sausage meat, finely chopped onion, egg and herbs, and put into pastry case. Cover with pastry lid, seal firmly, brush with beaten egg mixed with a pinch of salt, and bake at 425°F (Gas Mark 7) for 30 minutes. Cool completely.

Pack by wrapping in heavy-duty foil.

To serve: Thaw at room temperature for 3 hours.

Storage time: 1 month.

POTTED GROUSE

2 old grouse	Bunch of mixed
1 carrot	herbs
1 onion	Salt and pepper
2 oz. streaky bacon	Stock
Butter	

Slice carrot and onion and cut bacon in neat pieces, and fry in butter until golden. Put into the bottom of a casserole with the herbs, plenty of salt and pepper and the grouse. Cover with stock and cook at 300°F (Gas Mark 2) for 2½ hours. Remove carrot. Put meat from grouse with onion, bacon and a little stock through a mincer, then pound or liquidise to a smooth paste. A small glass of port may be added to this paste.

Pack in small containers with lids, or in foil containers covered with heavy-duty foil.

To serve: Thaw at room temperature for 1 hour.

Storage time: 1 month.

GROUSE CASSEROLE

2 grouse	Parsley, thyme and
8 oz. lean bacon	bay leaf
1 small onion	½ pint stock
1 carrot	1 wineglass red wine
1 stick celery	Salt and pepper

Flour the grouse very lightly and cook in a little butter until both sides are golden. Slice the bacon and vegetables. Take out grouse and put into casserole. Cook bacon and vegetables in butter until just soft, and add to casserole. Make sauce using the pan drippings and stock, thickening with a little cornflour (about 1 dsp). Season to taste with salt and pepper and pour over grouse. Cover and cook in low oven (325°F or Gas Mark 3) for 2 hours. Add wine and continue cooking for 30 minutes. Cool completely.

Pack in rigid plastic container.

To serve: Transfer to casserole and heat at 350°F (Gas Mark 4) for 45 minutes; split grouse in half and serve with vegetables and gravy and a garnish of watercress.

Storage time: 2 months.

PIGEON CASSEROLE

2 pigeons	Salt and pepper
8 oz. chuck steak	1 tbsp redcurrant
2 rashers bacon	jelly
½ pint stock	1 tbsp lemon juice
2 oz. small	1 tbsp cornflour
mushrooms	

Cut pigeons in halves and the steak in cubes, and cut bacon in small pieces. Cook pigeons, steak and bacon in a little butter until just coloured. Put into casserole with stock, sliced mushrooms, salt and pepper and cook at 325°F (Gas Mark 3) for 1 hour. Stir in red-currant jelly, lemon juice and cornflour blended with a little water, and continue cooking for 30 minutes. Cool.

Pack in foil-lined dish, forming foil into a parcel, and removing from dish when frozen for easy storage.

To serve: Heat at 350°F (Gas Mark 4) for 1 hour.

Storage time: 1 month.

PLUM COMPÔTE

1 lb ripe plums	1 wineglass sherry
½ pint water	or brandy
4 oz. sugar	

Stone the plums and poach gently in syrup made from water and sugar until fruit is just cooked but not broken. Stir in sherry or brandy and cool.

Pack in waxed or rigid plastic container.

To serve: Thaw in refrigerator for 3 hours and serve with thick cream.

Storage time: 2 months.

PLUM PUDDING

3 oz. butter	Pinch of salt
4 oz. sugar	2 eggs
6 oz. self-raising flour	8 oz. small plums

Cream butter and sugar and add eggs and flour by degrees, beating very thoroughly. Cut plums in half and remove stones, and toss lightly in a little extra sugar. Put a layer of batter in 2-lb foil basin, then a layer of plums, spaced to avoid touching. Pour over a layer of mixture, then plums, and repeat layers until all ingredients are used, finishing with a layer of batter. Cover with greaseproof paper and steam 1½ hours. Cool.

Pack by covering with a lid of heavy-duty foil.

To serve: Steam pudding for 1 hour, and serve with egg custard or cream.

Storage time: 2 months.

PEACH PUDDING

10 small peaches	2 oz. butter
2½ tbsp Demerara sugar	2 oz. sugar
	2 eggs
½ gill water	2 oz. plain flour

Stone the peaches and put in an oven dish which can be used in the freezer, or in a foil basin. Pour on water and Demerara sugar. Cream butter and sugar, add eggs and continue beating well, then gradually mix in flour. Pour over peaches and bake at 350°F (Gas Mark 4) for 1 hour, or steam for 1 hour. Cool.

Pack by covering with lid of heavy-duty foil.

To serve: Reheat at 325°F (Gas Mark 3), or steam for 45 minutes, and serve with cream.

Storage time: 2 months.

BLACKBERRY AND APPLE MOUSSE

1 lb. cooking apples	Juice of 1 lemon
8 oz. blackberries	½ oz. gelatine
¼ pint water	2 egg whites
4 oz. caster sugar	

Peel and slice the apples into a pan with the blackberries, water and 3 oz. sugar. Cover and simmer 15 minutes. Sprinkle lemon juice with gelatine and leave to soak. Take cooked fruit from heat, add gelatine and stir until dissolved. Put through a sieve, and leave purée to cool and thicken. Whisk egg whites stiffly, fold in remainder of sugar, and fold into fruit purée. Pour into a serving dish which can be used in the freezer, and leave until cold.

Pack by covering with a lid of heavy-duty foil.

To serve: Thaw in refrigerator for 3 hours, and decorate with cream.

Storage time: 2 months.

BLACKBERRY CAKE

4 oz. butter	*Topping:*
4 oz. sugar	8 oz. ripe black-
1 egg	berries
8 oz. plain flour	2 oz. butter
2 tsp baking	4 oz. sugar
powder	2 oz. flour
¼ tsp salt	½ tsp cinnamon
¼ pint milk	

Cream butter and sugar and beat in the egg. Gradually add flour sifted with baking powder and salt, and beat to a smooth batter with the milk. Pour into buttered rectangular tin (about 7 by 11 in.). Sprinkle thickly with well-washed and drained blackberries. Make a topping by creaming the butter and sugar and working in the flour and cinnamon to a crumbled consistency. Sprinkle on blackberries and bake at 350°F (Gas Mark 4) for 1 hour. Cool in tin.

Pack tin in polythene bag. A baking tin may be made from heavy-duty foil if it is not possible to spare one for the freezer.

To serve: Remove wrappings and thaw at room temperature for 2 hours. Cut in squares.

Storage time: 4 months.

LUNCHEON CAKE

4 oz. butter	2 tbsp milk
8 oz. caster sugar	2 tbsp honey
3 eggs	¼ tsp bicarbonate of
6 oz. plain flour	soda
½ tsp baking powder	8 oz. walnuts
¼ tsp salt	1 lb seedless raisins
½ tsp ground nutmeg	

Cream butter and sugar until light and fluffy. Beat eggs together and add to creamed mixture with sifted flour, baking powder, salt and nutmeg. Stir in milk. Mix honey and bicarbonate of soda together and add to mixture, and stir in walnuts and raisins. Put mixture into greased and floured 2-lb loaf tin. Bake at 325°F (Gas Mark 3) for 2¼ hours. Cool in tin before turning out.

Pack in polythene bag or heavy-duty foil.

To serve: Thaw in wrappings at room temperature for 3 hours.

Storage time: 4 months.

SEPTEMBER

This is the last chance for freezing most vegetables of good quality. There is the first game to enjoy, and the first casseroles and puddings to prepare ahead for colder days.

FOOD IN SEASON

Vegetables Aubergines, Brussels sprouts, cabbage, cauliflower, celery, corn-on-the-cob, courgettes, leeks, onions, parsnips, peppers, runner beans, spinach, swedes, tomatoes.
Fruit Apples, blackberries, damsons, grapes, peaches, pears, plums.
Fish Crab, haddock, halibut, herring, lobster, oysters, plaice, prawns, sole, turbot.
Meat, Poultry and Game Goose, turkey, grouse, hare, partridge, rabbit, snipe, venison, wild duck.

NOW IS THE TIME TO FREEZE:

Onions, parsnips, goose, partridge, rabbit, snipe, wild duck, woodcock, venison

ONIONS

Home-grown onions are best stored in strings. Those who like the flavour of imported onions may find them worth preserving for out-of-season use. A few packs of home-grown onions in the freezer can be useful to save time when making winter dishes. Onions to be served raw in salads should be cut in $\frac{1}{4}$-in. slices and packed in freezer paper or foil, with Cellophane dividing the slices, and the packages should be overwrapped to avoid cross-flavouring with other foods. These onions should be served while still frosty. Chopped onions for cooking should be blanched for 2 minutes, chilled, drained and packed in containers, then overwrapped. Very small whole onions which can later be served in a sauce can either be blanched for 4 minutes before freezing, or cooked until tender so that they need only to be reheated in a sauce or stew. It is important to label the onions carefully with the exact method used as a guide for further cooking. *Storage time:* 3 months.

PARSNIPS

Only freeze parsnips when they are young and small. If a quantity of older ones is available, the parsnips can be cooked and mashed before freezing. Trim small young parsnips and peel them, and remove any hard cores. Cut into narrow strips or ½-in. dice. Blanch for 2 minutes and pack in bags or rigid containers. *To serve:* Cook in boiling water for 15 minutes. *Storage time:* 1 year.

GOOSE

Goose for the freezer should be young and tender and not more than 12 lb in weight. A bird should be hung for 5 days before freezing. The bird should be plucked and drawn, with particular attention to removal of the oil glands. Giblets should be packed separately, and the bird should not be stuffed. *To serve:* Thaw in wrappings in refrigerator or cold larder, allowing 24–36 hours. At room temperature, a goose will take 6–8 hours. *Storage time:* 6–8 months.

PARTRIDGE

Partridges should be plucked and drawn before freezing, thoroughly cleaned, cooled and packed in polythene. It is best to pad the ends of the legs with a little foil or greaseproof paper to avoid tearing the outer wrapping. Old or badly shot birds are best cooked before freezing. *To serve:* Thaw in wrappings in the refrigerator, allowing 5 hours per lb, and cook as soon as the game has thawed and is still cold, to prevent loss of juices.

Storage time: 6–8 months.

RABBIT

Rabbits should be bled and hung for 24 hours in a cool place after shooting, and all shot wounds thoroughly cleaned. Skin and clean, washing the cavity well, and wipe with a damp cloth. It is best to cut rabbits into joints for neat packaging, and to wrap each piece in Cellophane or greaseproof paper, excluding air, then packing joints into polythene bags. *To serve:* Thaw in wrappings in refrigerator overnight before cooking. *Storage time:* 6–8 months.

SNIPE

Hang snipe for 3–4 days before preparing for the freezer. Pluck and remove crop, but do not draw. Pack in polythene, excluding air. *To serve:* Thaw in wrappings in the refrigerator, allowing 5 hours per lb, and cook as soon as thawed but still cold. *Storage time:* 6 months.

WILD DUCK

Hang for 1–3 days, pluck and draw. Be sure to remove oil-sacs from near the tail. Pack in polythene, excluding air. *To serve:* Thaw in wrappings in refrigerator, allowing 5 hours per lb, and cook as soon as thawed and still cold. *Storage time:* 6 months.

WOODCOCK

Hang for 3–4 days before freezing. Pluck and remove crop but do not draw. Pack in polythene, excluding air. *To serve:* Thaw in wrappings in the refrigerator, allowing 5 hours per lb, and cook as soon as thawed but still cold. *Storage time:* 6 months.

VENISON

A carcase of venison should be kept in good condition, the shot wounds carefully cleaned, and the animal kept as cold as possible. It should be beheaded and bled, skinned and cleaned, and the interior washed and wiped. The meat should then be hung in a very cool place (preferably just above freezing point) with the belly propped open so air can circulate. Seven to ten days' hanging will make the meat more tender. It should be wiped over on alternate days with milk to help keep the meat fresh. It is best to get a butcher to cut the meat, and it is wisest to keep only the best joints whole, packed in polythene with air excluded. Remaining meat can be minced to freeze raw for hamburgers or mince, or to casserole and make into pies. *To serve:* Pour over marinade which will prevent dryness, and thaw in a cool place, allowing 5 hours per lb. *Storage time:* 8–10 months.

Venison Marinade

Mix together ½ pint red wine, ½ pint vinegar, 1 large sliced lemon, parsley, thyme and a bay leaf. Pour over frozen venison joint as it thaws, turning meat frequently. Use the marinade for cooking the meat. For roasting, cover the meat with strips of fat bacon before cooking. Use loin and haunch for roasting; shoulder and neck for casseroles.

WHEN THERE'S A GLUT, FREEZE:

Apple Sauce, Apple Juice, Blackberry Jam

APPLE SAUCE

Cook apples to a pulp with a minimum of water. For the best flavour, this should be done in a casserole in the oven, using sliced but unpeeled apples. Sieve the sauce and sweeten to taste, adding a squeeze of lemon juice. Cool and pack into rigid containers, leaving $\frac{1}{2}$ in. headspace. *To serve:* Thaw for 3 hours at room temperature. *Storage time:* 1 year.

APPLE JUICE

Apple juice may be frozen, but should not be sweetened as fermentation sets in quickly. It is best made in the proportion of $\frac{1}{2}$ pint water to 2 lb apples, or it can be made by simmering leftover peelings in water. The juice should be strained through a jelly bag or cloth, and cooled completely before freezing. It may be frozen in a rigid container, leaving $\frac{1}{2}$ in. headspace, or in a loaf tin or ice-cube trays, the frozen blocks then being wrapped in foil or polythene for easy storage.

BLACKBERRY JAM

1½ lb blackberries   4 fl. oz. liquid pectin
2¾ lb caster sugar

This is best made with large cultivated black-berries, as the small hard wild ones are difficult to mash without liquid and are rather 'pippy'. Mash berries and stir in the sugar. Leave for 20 minutes, stirring occasionally, then add pectin and stir for 3 minutes. Pack in small or rigid plastic containers, cover tightly and seal. Leave at room temperature for 24–28 hours until jelled before freezing. *To serve:* Thaw at room temperature for 1 hour. *Storage time:* 1 year.

PREPARE-AHEAD DISHES

CARROT SOUP

1 lb carrots	3 large tomatoes
1 pint water	1 pint milk
1 oz. butter	

Scrape the carrots and cook for 30 minutes in water. Drain, reserving liquid, then grate carrots. Melt the butter and lightly cook skinned tomatoes. Add the grated carrot and cook until all the butter is absorbed. In a double saucepan, bring milk to the boil, add carrot and tomato, and liquid from carrots. Simmer for 45 minutes, seasoning lightly with salt and pepper. Cool.

Pack in waxed or rigid plastic container, leaving headspace.

To serve: Reheat gently in double boiler, adjusting seasoning, and garnish with toasted croutons and chopped parsley.

Storage time: 1 month.

LEEK SOUP

4 leeks	1 pint chicken stock
1 oz. butter	

Clean leeks thoroughly and cut into thin rings. Melt butter, and soften leeks without colouring them. Add stock, season lightly and simmer for 30 minutes. Cool.

Pack in waxed or rigid plastic container, leaving headspace.

To serve: Reheat gently, adjust seasoning, and stir in ¼ pint creamy milk. Garnish with chopped parsley or chives.

Storage time: 1 month.

STUFFED ONIONS

4 large onions	2 oz. fresh bread-
8 oz. cooked minced	crumbs
beef or lamb	¼ pint brown gravy
	1 tsp tomato purée

Peel the onions and boil until just tender. Remove centres and chop finely. Mix with meat, breadcrumbs and gravy, tomato purée, salt and pepper. Fill onions with this mixture and put into a baking tin with a little dripping. Sprinkle with a few breadcrumbs and bake at 400°F (Gas Mark 6) for 45 minutes, basting well. Cool.

Pack in foil tray, covering with lid of heavy-duty foil.

To serve: Heat at 350°F (Gas Mark 4) for 45 minutes and serve with gravy.

Storage time: 1 month.

PARTRIDGE AND MUSHROOMS

2 partridges	1½ oz. flour
8 oz. small	¾ pint stock
mushrooms	¼ pint sherry
2 oz. butter	Salt and pepper

Clean the partridges. Wipe the mushrooms and cook gently in a little of the butter for 5 minutes. Lightly salt and pepper and leave to cool. Stuff partridges with mushrooms and put in pan with remaining butter. Cover pan and allow birds to brown. Remove birds from fat. Work in the flour, then the stock and sherry, and simmer for 5 minutes. Put in the partridges and simmer for 40 minutes. Cool completely.

Pack in waxed or rigid plastic containers, covering birds with sauce.

To serve: Put into casserole and heat at 325°F (Gas Mark 3) for 45 minutes, adjusting seasoning to taste. Garnish with watercress.

Storage time: 2 months.

DEEP CHICKEN PIE

1 boiling chicken	Pinch of mixed herbs
3 rashers bacon	Salt and pepper
1 tbsp chopped parsley	12 oz. short pastry

Boil the chicken for about 3 hours until tender. Take flesh from the bones and put in layers in a foil pie-dish, alternating with finely chopped bacon and parsley and a sprinkling of mixed herbs. Season lightly and cover with a gravy made from the chicken stock thickened with a little cornflour. Cool and cover with pastry. Bake at 450°F (Gas Mark 8) for 45 minutes. Cool completely.

Pack by putting foil dish into polythene bag.

To serve: Reheat at 350°F (Gas Mark 4) for 45 minutes. Pie may be frozen with uncooked pastry, and should then be baked straight from freezer at 450°F (Gas Mark 8) for 1 hour.

Storage time: 2 months.

RABBIT CASSEROLE

1 rabbit	⅓ pint cider
4 oz. fat bacon	Parsley, thyme and
2 large onions	bay leaf
1 pint stock	

Divide rabbit into joints. Cut bacon into small pieces and heat until the fat runs. Cut onions in thin slices. Fry rabbit joints and onions in the bacon fat until lightly coloured brown. Sprinkle lightly with flour and season well with salt and pepper. Add stock and cider, herbs and bacon pieces, and simmer for 45 minutes. Cool.

Pack in waxed or rigid plastic container.

To serve: Return to casserole and simmer for 45 minutes, and garnish with chopped parsley.

Storage time: 2 months.

LAMB IN CIDER

2 lb lamb shoulder	¼ pint stock
(without bone)	¼ pint cider
2 oz. butter	1 tbsp Worcester-
2 small onions	shire sauce
1 small garlic clove	Salt and pepper
2 tbsp parsley	

Cut meat into cubes and coat lightly with flour. Fry in the butter until brown on all sides. Put in casserole with chopped onion, garlic and parsley. Heat stock and cider together, add sauce and seasoning and simmer for 5 minutes. Pour over meat, cover and simmer at 325°F (Gas Mark 3) for 45 minutes. Cool.

Pack in waxed or rigid plastic container.

To serve: Return to casserole and heat at

325°F (Gas Mark 3) for 45 minutes.
Storage time: 2 months.

BRAISED BEEF

1 lb mixed vegetables (carrots, onions, celery, leeks, turnips)	2 oz. lard or dripping
	Salt and pepper
	Parsley, thyme and bay leaf
3 lb rolled rib beef	Water or stock

Peel vegetables and cut into neat cubes to make a layer 2 in. thick in a pan which will just fit the beef. Fry the meat in the fat until browned on all sides, and put on top of the vegetables. Add seasoning and herbs, and pour in hot water or stock to a depth of about 1 in. Cover and cook at 325°F (Gas Mark 3) for 1½ hours. Cool.

Pack in waxed or rigid plastic container.

To serve: Return to casserole and heat at 325°F (Gas Mark 3) for 1 hour.

Storage time: 2 months.

PEARS IN RED WINE

8 eating pears	¼ pint Burgundy
8 oz. sugar	2 in. cinnamon stick
¼ pint water	

Peel pears, but leave whole with stalks on. Dissolve sugar in water and add cinnamon stick. Simmer pears in syrup with lid on for 15 minutes then add Burgundy and cover the pan. Continue simmering for 15 minutes. Drain pears and put into individual leak-proof containers. Reduce syrup by boiling until it is thick, then pour over pears, and cool.

Pack in leak-proof containers since the syrup does not freeze solid; the pears lose moisture on thawing and thin the syrup, but the effect is lessened if they are packed in individual containers.

To serve: Thaw in refrigerator for 8 hours.

Storage time: 2 months.

BAKED APPLE DUMPLINGS

8 apples	Butter
Sugar	8 oz. short pastry

Core apples, leaving $\frac{1}{4}$ in. core at bottom of each to hold filling. Fill with sugar and put a knob of butter in each. Put each apple on a square of pastry and seal joins. Bake at 425°F (Gas Mark 7) for 25 minutes. Cool.

Pack into container or foil dish with lid of heavy-duty foil.

To serve: Heat at 375°F (Gas Mark 5) while still frozen for 20 minutes, and serve with cream, custard or hot apricot jam.

Storage time: 1 month.

CANADIAN APPLE PIE

12 oz. short pastry	Pinch each of
1 lb apples	cloves, ginger and
Sugar	cinnamon
Juice of $\frac{1}{2}$ lemon	4 oz. mixed dried
	fruit

Line a pie plate with short pastry. Cover with a layer of sliced apple, sprinkle with sugar and lemon juice, spices and dried fruit. Put on another layer of apples, then other ingredients, and finish with a layer of apples. Cover with pastry. Bake at 450°F (Gas Mark 8) for 15 minutes, then at 400°F (Gas Mark 6) for 25 minutes. Cool.

Pack by wrapping in polythene or heavy-duty foil.

To serve: Thaw at room temperature for 3 hours, or reheat in low oven to serve hot, with cream or egg custard.

APPLE CRUMBLE

1½ lb apples	*Topping:*
1 tbsp water	3 oz. plain flour
½ oz. butter	2 oz. butter
3 oz. brown sugar	1 oz. caster sugar
Pinch of mixed spice	

Peel and slice apples and simmer very gently with water and butter for 15 minutes. Stir in sugar and spice, and put into oven-dish which will go in the freezer, or into foil dish. Rub butter into flour and work in the sugar until mixture is like large crumbs. Spoon over the fruit and press down lightly. Bake at 350°F (Gas Mark 4) for 30 minutes. Cool.

Pack by covering with polythene or heavy-duty foil lid.

To serve: Heat at 350°F (Gas Mark 4) for 40 minutes, and serve with cream or egg custard.

Storage time: 2 months.

BLACKBERRY SAUCE

8 oz. blackberries	2 tsp cornflour
6 tbsp cold water	1 tsp lemon juice
2 oz. caster sugar	

Put blackberries in a pan with 1 tbsp water. Simmer for 10 minutes and add sugar. Put through a sieve. Mix cornflour with remaining water and pour in blackberry purée. Heat gently until mixture thickens and comes to the boil. Remove from heat, stir in lemon juice and cool.

Pack in waxed or rigid plastic container.

To serve: Heat gently in double boiler and use with steamed puddings, milk puddings or ice cream.

Storage time: 2 months.

BROWN BREAD ICE

8 oz. brown bread- crumbs	½ pint double cream
4 tbsp Maraschino or Creme de Noyau	2 fl. oz. white rum or brandy

Mix all the ingredients well together and freeze to a semi-solid consistency. Beat well and freeze 1½ hours.

Pack in waxed or rigid plastic container.

To serve: Scoop out into small bowls.

Storage time: 2 months.

MOCHA CAKE

4 oz. self-raising
  flour
Pinch of salt
3 eggs
4 oz. caster sugar
2 oz. butter

Icing:
4 oz. butter
2 tsp coffee essence
6 oz. icing sugar
3 oz. chopped
  browned almonds

Sift together flour and salt. Melt butter slowly.
Boil some water in a large saucepan, remove
from heat, and put a bowl over the hot water.
In bowl, break the eggs, add the sugar and
whisk together for 5 minutes until pale and
thick. Remove basin from pan and continue
whisking until cold. Add melted butter, flour
and salt, and fold in until well mixed. Put into
a lined 6-in. square tin. Bake at 350°F (Gas
Mark 4) for 40 minutes. Cool. Make the icing
by beating butter until soft and gradually
working in the sugar until fluffy. Beat in the
coffee essence. Cut cake in half, spread with a
thin layer of icing, and put cake together.
Spread remaining icing on top of cake and
sprinkle with nuts.

Pack cake in polythene or foil *after* freezing.

To serve: Remove from wrappings and
thaw at room temperature for 3 hours.

Storage time: 2 months.

OCTOBER

This is a good time to freeze winter greens and root vegetables, and game. Grapes and pears are good value to freeze for fruit salads. The cheaper cuts of meat can be turned into casseroles for future meals, when time is occupied by Christmas shopping and preparations.

FOOD IN SEASON

Vegetables Brussels sprouts, cabbage, celery, leeks, parsnips, spinach, swedes, turnips.
Fruit Apples, blackberries, damsons, grapes, nuts, pears, pomegranates, pumpkin, quinces.
Fish Cod, haddock, herring, mackerel, oysters, plaice, scallops, sole, sprats, turbot.
Meat, Poultry and Game Grouse, hare, partridge, pheasant, snipe, venison, wild duck.

NOW IS THE TIME TO FREEZE:

Brussels sprouts, celery, swedes, turnips, pomegranates, grapes, nuts, quinces, pheasant

BRUSSELS SPROUTS

Freeze only small compact heads of Brussels sprouts, and do not over-blanch them or they will be soggy and smell unpleasant. Grade heads for size before blanching. Remove discoloured leaves and wash well. Blanch 3 minutes for small sprouts, 4 minutes for medium sprouts. Cool and pack in cartons or bags. *To serve:* Cook for 8 minutes in boiling water. *Storage time:* 1 year.

CELERY

Celery cannot be used raw after freezing, but it is useful to freeze for future stews and soups, or as a vegetable. Use crisp tender stalks and remove any strings. Scrub well and remove all grit and dirt under running water. Cut in 1-in. lengths and blanch for 3 minutes. Pack dry in polythene bags or in boxes, or use rigid containers and cover with the flavoured liquid in which the celery has been blanched, leaving $\frac{1}{2}$ in. headspace. This liquid can be used with the celery in soups or stews. *To serve:* Simmer in freezing liquid for 10 minutes, or braise dry celery in stock. Celery frozen in liquid can be added to soups and stews while still frozen. *Storage time:* 1 year.

SWEDES

Prepare swedes for the freezer while still young. They are best prepared as purée. Cook swedes until tender in the minimum of water, drain, mash and freeze in rigid containers, leaving ½ in. headspace. *To serve:* Reheat gently with butter and seasoning. *Storage time:* 1 year.

TURNIPS

Turnips should only be frozen when small, young and mild-flavoured. They are best sliced or diced, or prepared as a purée. Trim and peel small mild turnips, and cut into slices or ½-in. dice. Blanch for 2½ minutes, cool and pack in rigid containers. Mashed turnips can be prepared by cooking until tender, draining, mashing and freezing in rigid containers, leaving ½ in. headspace. *To serve:* Cook turnips in boiling water for 10 minutes. Reheat purée gently with butter and seasoning. *Storage time:* 1 year.

POMEGRANATES

Pomegranate juice is worth freezing for use in drinks or fruit salads, and the fruit is also useful for fruit salads. To freeze the juice, extract with a lemon squeezer, sweeten to taste, and freeze in small containers or ice-cube trays, each frozen cube then being wrapped in foil for storage. To use the fruit, cut fully ripe fruit in half, scoop out the red juice sacs, and pack them in 50% syrup (16 oz. sugar to 1 pint water) in small containers. *To serve:* Thaw at room temperature for 3 hours. *Storage time:* 1 year.

GRAPES

These are very useful to serve in winter fruit salads or jellies, and they can be packed in small quantities. Choose firm, ripe grapes which are sweet and have tender skins. White varieties have a better flavour for freezing. Seedless varieties can be packed whole, but others should be skinned and pipped and cut in half. They are best packed in 30% syrup (7 oz. sugar to 1 pint water). *To serve:* Thaw at room temperature for 2½ hours. *Storage time:* 1 year. A perfect bunch of grapes can be frozen to use for a dessert bowl, and will keep for 2 weeks. The bunch should be put into a polythene bag to freeze. The grapes will look full and rich, and will taste delicious, but will deteriorate quickly after thawing.

NUTS

All kinds of nuts can be frozen and they will keep moist and fresh. They can be frozen whole, chopped, slivered, or buttered and toasted, but they should not be salted. Small containers, foil or polythene bags can be used, and they should be thawed in wrappings at room temperature for 3 hours. *Storage time:* 1 year (4 months if buttered and toasted).

QUINCES

Quinces have a distinctive flavour which is retained well in the freezer. Wash fruit well, peel and core. The peelings (but not the cores) should be simmered in a pan with water to cover and the juice of 1 orange and 1 lemon, until the peel is tender. The sliced quinces should be cooked in the strained liquid until tender, removed from heat, and $1\frac{1}{2}$ lb sugar added for each 2 lb of prepared quinces. When the sugar has dissolved and the mixture has cooled, strain off the syrup and chill. Pack the quince slices into waxed or rigid containers, pour over the syrup and cover, leaving $\frac{1}{2}$ in. headspace. *To serve:* Thaw the quinces at room temperature for 3 hours. *Storage time:* 1 year.

PHEASANT

Pheasant should be plucked and drawn before freezing, after hanging for 7–10 days. Birds hung after freezing and thawing will deteriorate rapidly. Pack in polythene, excluding air, and padding protruding bones. Old or badly shot birds are best used in a casserole, pie or pâté which can be frozen. *To serve:* Thaw pheasant in refrigerator, allowing 5 hours per lb and start cooking as soon as thawed and still cold to prevent loss of juices. *Storage time:* 6–8 months.

PREPARE-AHEAD DISHES

ONION SOUP

1½ lb onions   Salt and pepper
2 oz. butter   2 tbsp cornflour
3 pints beef stock

Slice the onions finely and cook gently in butter until soft and golden. Add stock and seasoning, bring to the boil, and simmer for 20 minutes. Thicken with cornflour and simmer for 5 minutes.

Pack after cooling and removing fat, into containers, leaving headspace.

To serve: Reheat in double boiler, stirring gently. Meanwhile, spread slices of French bread with butter and grated cheese, and toast until cheese has melted. Put slices into tureen or individual bowls and pour over soup.

Storage time: 2 months.

OXTAIL SOUP

1 oxtail	1 turnip
2½ pints water	1 stick celery
2 carrots	Salt
2 onions	

Wipe oxtail and cut in pieces. Toss in a little seasoned flour and fry in a little butter for 10 minutes. Put in pan with water and simmer for 2 hours. Remove meat from bones and return to stock with vegetables cut in neat pieces. Simmer for 45 minutes and put through a sieve, or liquidise. Cool and remove fat.

Pack in containers, leaving headspace.

To serve: Reheat gently in saucepan, adding ½ tsp Worcestershire sauce and ½ tsp lemon juice.

Storage time: 2 months.

PHEASANT IN CIDER

1 old pheasant	1 garlic clove
1 lb cooking apples	Bunch of mixed
8 oz. onions	herbs
½ pint cider	Salt and pepper

Clean and wipe pheasant. Cut apples in quarters after peeling and coring, and put into a casserole. Slice onions and cook until soft in a little butter. Put pheasant on to apples and cover with onions. Pour on cider and add crushed garlic and herbs and season with salt and pepper. Cover and cook at 325°F (Gas Mark 3) for 2 hours. Cool and remove herbs.

Pack in foil container and strain sauce over pheasant. Cover with foil lid. Or pack in foil-lined casserole, removing and sealing foil parcel after freezing for easy storage.

To serve: Put into casserole, and cook at 350°F (Gas Mark 4) for 1 hour.

Storage time: 1 month.

PHEASANT PÂTÉ

8 oz. calves' liver	1 large cooked
4 oz. bacon	pheasant
1 small onion	Powdered cloves and
Salt and pepper	allspice

Cook liver and bacon lightly in a little butter and put through a mincer with the onion. Season with salt and pepper. Remove meat from pheasant in neat pieces and season lightly with cloves and allspice. Put a layer of liver mixture into a dish (foil pie dish, loaf tin, or terrine), and add a layer of pheasant. Continue in layers finishing with liver mixture. Cover and steam for 2 hours. Cool with heavy weights on top.

Pack by covering container with foil lid and sealing with freezer tape, or by turning pâté out of cooking utensil and wrapping in heavy-duty foil.

To serve: Thaw in wrappings in refrigerator for 6 hours, or at room temperature for 3 hours.

Storage time: 1 month.

PARTRIDGE PUDDING

2 partridges	Pinch of Cayenne
1 lb rump steak	pepper
8 oz. lean ham	Gravy
4 oz. mushrooms	8 oz. self-raising
1 tsp salt	flour
½ tsp pepper	4 oz. shredded suet
1 saltspoon mace	Salt and pepper

146

Roast the partridges for 30 minutes and cut them up, removing skin and bones. Cut steak into cubes, and slice ham and mushrooms. Mix with seasonings. Mix flour and suet, season lightly with salt and pepper, and mix with enough cold water to make a soft dough. Line a foil pudding basin with two-thirds of the dough, and put in meat mixture. Add some brown gravy or stock to just cover the meat. Cover with remaining suet pastry. Cover and steam for 4 hours. Cool completely.

Pack by covering basin with heavy-duty foil lid, or by putting basin in polythene bag.

To serve: Steam for $1\frac{1}{2}$ hours.

Storage time: 2 months.

COUNTRY PORK CHOPS

4 spare rib pork chops	1 oz. fat
1 clove garlic	Salt, pepper and nutmeg
$1\frac{1}{2}$ lb potatoes	4 oz. bacon
1 onion	3 fl. oz. cider

Put a sliver of garlic into each pork chop. Brown the chops in the fat. Cut potatoes and onion in thin slices. Put half the potatoes and onion in an oven dish which can be used in the freezer, or in a foil dish. Season with salt, pepper and nutmeg, and put chops on top. Cover with remaining potatoes and onion, and season again. Cover with bacon cut in small pieces, pour over cider, cover with a lid and cook at 300°F (Gas Mark 2) for 2 hours. Cool and pour off surplus fat.

Pack by covering dish with a heavy-duty foil lid.

To serve: Heat at 350°F (Gas Mark 4) for
1 hour without a lid.

Storage time: 1 month.

APPLE SHORTCAKE

6 oz. self-raising flour	3 oz. caster sugar
Pinch of salt	1 egg
4 oz. butter	1 lb apples
	Sugar for apples

Peel and slice apples and cook with sugar to
taste and very little water. Cool. Sift flour and
salt. Cream butter and sugar, and stir in flour
and beaten egg. Leave in a cool place for 10
minutes to become firm. Grease 7-in. sandwich tin and put strips of greaseproof paper
at right angles across base and up the sides so
that the shortcake can be lifted out easily. Line
base with greased greaseproof paper. Divide
pastry into halves, and roll out each piece to
7 in. round. Put one round in tin, prick with
a fork and cover with apple. Cover with
second round and prick lightly. Bake at 325°F
(Gas Mark 3) for 1 hour. Cool.

Pack by removing from tin and wrapping in
heavy-duty foil.

To serve: Thaw at room temperature for 3
hours, dust with caster sugar and serve with
cream.

Storage time: 2 months.

BAKEWELL TART

8 oz. puff pastry
4 oz. jam
4 oz. butter
4 oz. caster sugar

2 eggs
4 oz. ground
   almonds

Line pie plate or foil dish with pastry and spread with jam. Melt the butter, stir in sugar, then beaten eggs and almonds. Beat well and put over jam. Bake at 350°F (Gas Mark 4) for 40 minutes. Cool.

Pack in foil or polythene bags.

To serve: Thaw in loose wrappings at room temperature for 3 hours.

Storage time: 2 months.

PLUM UPSIDE-DOWN PUDDING

2 oz. butter
4 oz. soft brown
   sugar
12 oz. plums

3 eggs
3 oz. caster sugar
3 oz. plain flour

Melt butter and brown sugar over gentle heat. Pour into oven dish which will go in the freezer, or into foil dish. Halve and stone the plums and place cut side down on the melted mixture. Whisk eggs and sugar in a bowl over gently steaming water for 10 minutes. Fold in sieved flour. Pour over plums. Cook at 375°F (Gas Mark 5) for 35 minutes. Cool.

Pack by covering dish with heavy-duty foil lid.

To serve: Thaw at room temperature for 3 hours, and heat at 325°F (Gas Mark 3) for 30 minutes. Turn out and serve with cream.

Storage time: 2 months.

NUT ICE CREAM

6 oz. mixed nuts (walnuts, almonds, hazels, brazils)	Pinch of salt
	1 pint cream
	2 eggs
6 oz. caster sugar	1 tsp vanilla essence

Blanch and chop nuts fairly finely. Mix sugar, salt and nuts and add the cream gradually. Put in a double boiler and cook over hot water for 10 minutes. Remove from stove and stir in the beaten eggs very slowly. Freeze to a mush, beat and return to freezer until firm. This ice is also delicious if coffee essence is used instead of vanilla (use 2 tsp).

Pack in waxed or rigid plastic container.

To serve: Scoop into small dishes and serve with sweet wafers.

Storage time: 1 year.

APPLE SULTAN SORBET

1½ lb cooking apples	*Compôte:*
6 oz. caster sugar	8 oz. sultanas
Peel of 1 lemon	½ pint water
1 in. cinnamon stick	1 oz. white rum
1 pint water	3 oz. caster sugar
Juice of 2 lemons	1 bay leaf
Green vegetable colouring	Strip of lemon peel
2 fl. oz. brandy	
¼ pint double cream	

Peel and slice apples, and put into pan with sugar, lemon peel, cinnamon and water. Cook until apples are tender, add lemon juice, and colour lightly green. Put through a sieve, cool and add brandy. Freeze to a thick batter, add whipped cream and continue freezing for 1½ hours. Make compôte by simmering all ingredients together until like thick cream, removing bay leaf and lemon peel, and chilling compôte before using with the apple ice (or freezing it in a separate container).

Pack both apple ice and sultana compôte in separate waxed or rigid plastic containers.

To serve: Thaw compôte in refrigerator for 3 hours, and serve over apple ice.

Storage time: 1 year.

WALNUT BREAD

12 oz. self-raising wholemeal flour	6 oz. chopped walnuts
½ tsp salt	2 beaten eggs
8 oz. Barbados sugar	8 fl. oz. milk
	2 oz. melted butter

Stir together flour, salt and sugar. Add walnuts, beaten eggs, milk and butter. Beat well together, leave to stand for 20 minutes, then put into a tin lined with greaseproof paper (about 9 by 5 by 3 in.). Bake at 350°F (Gas Mark 4) for 1 hour 10 minutes until firm. Cool.

Pack in heavy-duty foil or polythene.

To serve: Thaw at room temperature for 3 hours, slice and spread with butter and honey.

Storage time: 2 months.

APPLE CAKE

4 oz. self-raising wholemeal flour	2 oz. butter
Pinch of salt	1 egg
3 oz. Barbados sugar	1 lb crisp eating apples

Sieve flour and salt. Cream sugar and butter together until light and fluffy and beat in egg. Peel and core apples and cut in fine slices. Add flour and apples to butter mixture and put into greased 7-in. cake tin. Bake at 375°F (Gas Mark 5) for 45 minutes until golden brown. Cool on rack.

Pack in heavy-duty foil or polythene.

To serve: Thaw at room temperature for 3 hours and sprinkle with brown sugar.

Storage time: 2 months.

GINGERBREAD

8 oz. golden syrup	1 tsp ground ginger
2 oz. butter	1 oz. candied peel
2 oz. sugar	1 tsp bicarbonate of
1 egg	soda
8 oz. plain flour	Milk

Melt syrup over low heat with butter and sugar, and gradually add to sifted flour and ginger together with beaten egg. Mix bicarbonate of soda with a little milk and beat into the mixture, and add chopped peel. Pour into rectangular tin and bake at 325°F (Gas Mark 3) for 1 hour. Cool in tin.

Pack baking tin into polythene bag or heavy-duty foil, or cut gingerbread in squares and pack in polythene bags or boxes.

To serve: Thaw in wrappings at room temperature for 2 hours. This cake may be served as a pudding with apple purée and cream or ice cream.

Storage time: 2 months.

NOVEMBER

There is little worth freezing in the way of fresh raw materials, except game, but this is the time to stock the freezer with Christmas foods, and to supplement the bulk buying list with a few party specialities if time is short.

FOOD IN SEASON

Vegetables Brussels sprouts, cabbage, celery, Jerusalem artichokes, leeks, parsnips, swedes, turnips.
Fruit Apples, cranberries, grapes, pears, pomegranates, tangerines.
Fish Cod, haddock, herring, mackerel, oysters, plaice, scallops, sole, sprats, turbot, whiting.
Meat, Poultry and Game Goose, turkey, hare, partridge, pheasant, snipe, wild duck.

BULK BUYING CHECKLIST

Cream, ice cream, prepared party dishes (e.g. pâté, potted shrimps), poultry, bacon, sausages.

NOW IS THE TIME TO FREEZE:

Tangerines, persimmons

TANGERINES

Divide tangerines into sections, removing all pith. Pack in dry sugar, allowing 8 oz. sugar to 3 breakfast cups of tangerine segments, and pack in containers or polythene bags. Sections may also be packed in 30% syrup (7 oz. sugar to 1 pint water) in waxed or rigid plastic containers, covering with Cellophane and leaving ½ in. headspace. *To serve:* Thaw 2½ hours at room temperature. *Storage time:* 1 year.

PERSIMMONS

These fruit may be frozen whole and raw, or packed in syrup, or as purée. Whole unpeeled fruit should be wrapped in foil for freezing, and will take 3 hours to thaw at room temperature. Fruit should be used when barely thawed, as it darkens and loses flavour when left standing after freezing. *Storage time:* 2 months. Fully ripe fruit should be peeled and frozen whole in 50% syrup (16 oz. sugar to 1 pint water), with the addition of 1 dsp lemon juice to 1 quart syrup. Purée may be sweetened, allowing 8 oz. sugar to 4 breakfast cups of purée. *Storage time:* 1 year.

PREPARE-AHEAD DISHES

HARE SOUP

1 hare	Salt and pepper
1 lb lean ham	3 blades of mace
3 medium onions	6 pints beef stock
Parsley, thyme and	2 rolls
marjoram	$\frac{1}{2}$ pint port

Cut hare into joints and put into a pan with chopped ham and onions, herbs, salt and pepper, mace and stock. Simmer for $2\frac{1}{2}$ hours. Remove meat from bones and put into a blender with the ham, the crumbled rolls and some of the hare liquor which has been strained. Blend until smooth, then mix with remaining hare liquor and port, and simmer for 20 minutes. Cool.

Pack in waxed or rigid plastic containers, leaving headspace.

To serve: Reheat gently in double boiler.

Storage time: 2 months.

PRESSED OX TONGUE

1 ox tongue	Parsley, thyme and
1 carrot	bay leaf
1 onion	10 peppercorns
2 sticks celery	

Soak the tongue overnight if it has been salted. Put in a large pan with cold water and bring slowly to the boil. Drain tongue, cover with fresh water and bring to the boil again. Add chopped carrot, onion, celery, bunch of herbs and peppercorns. Cover and simmer for 3 hours. Cool in the liquid, then remove bones, fat and gristle and skin. Curl tongue into a round cake tin or soufflé dish and cover with weights. Leave in a cold place for 12 hours.

Pack tongue in freezer paper and overwrap with polythene.

To serve: Thaw in refrigerator overnight.

Storage time: 2 months.

STEAK AND KIDNEY PUDDING

12 oz. self-raising flour	1½ gills cold water
¼ tsp salt	1½ lb chuck steak
4½ oz. suet	½ lb ox kidney
	Salt and pepper

Mix flour and salt, stir in suet and mix to a soft but not sticky dough with water. Cut steak and kidney into pieces and toss in a little flour lightly seasoned with salt and pepper. Use two-thirds of the suet pastry to line a large foil basin (about 2½-pint size). Put in meat and half fill with cold water. Cover with a lid of pastry and seal edges. Cover with greased greaseproof paper and steam for 3 hours. Cool.

Pack by covering basin with lid of heavy-duty foil.

To serve: Steam for 1½ hours.

Storage time: 2 months.

BEEF IN WINE

3 lb shin beef	2 oz. bacon
1½ oz. butter	Thyme and parsley
1½ oz. oil	1 tbsp tomato purée
1 medium onion	Stock
2 garlic cloves	½ pint red wine

Cut meat into slices and cover very lightly with seasoned flour. Fry in a mixture of butter and oil until meat is just coloured, then add sliced onion, crushed garlic and bacon cut in small strips. Add herbs and wine and cook quickly until liquid is reduced to half. Work in tomato purée and just cover in stock, then simmer for 2 hours. Remove herbs and cool.

Pack into waxed or rigid plastic containers, or into foil-lined dish, forming the foil into a parcel, and removing for storage when frozen.

To serve: Reheat in a double boiler.

Storage time: 2 months.

PHEASANT IN WINE

2 young pheasants	4 oz. small
12 small onions	mushrooms
2 tbsp oil	1 pint Burgundy
2 tbsp butter	1 oz. plain flour
	Salt and pepper

Clean the pheasants. Chop two of the onions with the birds' livers and put half the mixture in each bird. Heat oil and butter together and brown birds all over. Put into a casserole. Remove mushroom stalks and cook in the remaining fat with the wine, until liquid is reduced by half. Mix flour with a little butter and use this to thicken the gravy and pour over the pheasants. Cook onions in boiling salted water until tender, drain and add to casserole. Toss mushrooms in butter and add to other ingredients. Cover and cook at 325°F (Gas Mark 3) for 1 hour. Cool.

Pack in rigid plastic container.

To serve: Return to casserole and reheat at 325°F (Gas Mark 3) for 1 hour. Serve with triangles of fried bread, and garnish with watercress.

Storage time: 2 months.

SALMON ROLLS

8 oz. short pastry
2 tbsp white sauce
1 tsp lemon juice

8-oz. tin pink
    salmon
Salt and pepper

Roll pastry into a long narrow strip about 3 in.
wide. Mix white sauce, lemon juice and drained
salmon and season well. Place the mixture
along one side of the pastry and roll up to
enclose the filling. Cut across in 3-in. lengths.
Brush with a little beaten egg and bake at
350°F (Gas Mark 4) for 10 minutes. Cool.

Pack in foil trays inside polythene bags.

To serve: Thaw at room temperature for 1
hour to serve cold, or heat in a low oven (325°F
or Gas Mark 3) for 20 minutes.

Storage time: 1 month.

YARMOUTH STRAWS

6 oz. short pastry
1 beaten egg
1 tbsp grated
    Parmesan

1 large cooked
    kipper

Roll out pastry into two 3-in. strips. Brush one
strip with beaten egg, and sprinkle half the
cheese on the other piece. Remove bones from
kipper and pound the flesh. Put kipper on one
piece of pastry, cover with the other piece and
sprinkle on remaining cheese. Cut into $\frac{3}{4}$-in.
fingers. Bake at 350°F (Gas Mark 4) for 10
minutes. Cool.

Pack in foil trays inside polythene bags.

To serve: Reheat at 325°F (Gas Mark 3) for
20 minutes.

RUM BABAS

6 oz. self-raising
  flour
Pinch of salt
2 oz. butter
3 oz. caster sugar
2 eggs
2 tbsp milk

Syrup:
4 oz. granulated
  sugar
$\frac{1}{2}$ pint water
4 tbsp rum
1 tbsp lemon juice

Sift flour and salt. Cream butter and sugar, and beat in eggs one at a time, adding a little flour with each. Beat in milk with a little more flour, then stir in remaining flour. Divide mixture into twelve individual baba rings, or one large ring tin. Bake at 375°F (Gas Mark 5) for 15 minutes (25 minutes for large one). Cool on a rack. Make syrup by dissolving sugar in water, boiling without stirring for 10 minutes, then adding rum and lemon juice. Prick warm babas with a skewer and pour over hot syrup, basting well. Cool.

Pack in rigid plastic container.

To serve: Remove from container and thaw at room temperature for 3 hours. Sprinkle with a little rum and serve with thick cream.

Storage time: 3 months.

CRANBERRY PIE

6 oz. short pastry
$\frac{1}{4}$ pint water
6 oz. soft brown
  sugar

8 oz. fresh cran-
  berries
1 tsp cornflour
1 oz. butter

Line a pie plate or foil dish with half the pastry. Dissolve sugar in water, and add cranberries. Simmer for 10 minutes until skins pop and fruit is soft. Blend cornflour with a little water, stir into cranberries and bring to the boil, stirring until thickened. Remove from heat and add butter. Pour filling into pastry case and cover with remaining pastry. Brush with milk and bake at 400°F (Gas Mark 6) for 30 minutes. Cool.

Pack by wrapping in heavy-duty foil or polythene.

To serve: Reheat at 325°F (Gas Mark 3) for 30 minutes and sprinkle with sugar. Serve with cream.

Storage time: 2 months.

ORANGE SORBET

2 tsp gelatine	1 tsp grated orange
½ pint water	rind
6 oz. sugar	½ pint orange juice
1 tsp grated lemon	4 tbsp lemon juice
rind	2 egg whites

Soak gelatine in a little of the water and boil the rest of the water and sugar for 10 minutes to a syrup. Stir gelatine into syrup and cool. Add rinds and juices. Beat egg whites until stiff but not dry and fold into mixture. Freeze to a mush, beat once, then continue freezing, allowing 3 hours' total freezing time. This ice will not go completely hard.

Pack in waxed or rigid plastic containers.

To serve: Scoop into bowls, or into fresh fruit cases (see below).

Storage time: 1 year.

Lemon Sorbet Follow the same method, using only lemon juice and rind to make up the total quantities, instead of a mixture of orange and lemon.

Fresh Fruit Cases Orange and lemon sorbets are particularly attractive if packed into fruit skins. Scoop out the oranges or lemons, wash thoroughly and dry and pack in sorbet when it is ready for storage, leaving surface raised above fruit skins. Wrap containers in foil for storage. If this is not done before storage, the skins may be prepared and left wet and the sorbet packed in and returned unwrapped to the freezer for 1 hour before serving.

ORANGE CREAM ICE

3 oranges	5 egg yolks
½ pint creamy milk	¼ pint double cream
2½ oz. caster sugar	

Peel the oranges very thinly and put peel in a pan with the milk and sugar. Boil gently for 10 minutes. Pour on to egg yolks, and stir gently until mixture thickens without boiling (this is best done in a double saucepan or in a bowl over hot water). Put through a sieve and cool. Add the strained juice of the oranges, and freeze this custard to the consistency of batter. Add whipped cream and continue freezing for 1½ hours.

Pack in waxed or rigid plastic containers, or into orange skins.

To serve: Scoop into small bowls and serve with sweet biscuits. This ice may also be served in hollowed-out orange skins (see ORANGE SORBET).

Storage time: 1 year.

CRANBERRY SAUCE

1 lb cranberries   ¾ lb sugar
¾ pint water

Rinse the cranberries. Dissolve sugar in water over gentle heat. Add cranberries and cook gently for 15 minutes until cranberries pop. Cool.

Pack in small waxed containers.

To serve: Thaw at room temperature for 3 hours.

Storage time: 1 year.

CRANBERRY ORANGE RELISH

1 lb fresh cranberries   1 lb sugar
2 large oranges

Mince together cranberries and orange flesh, and stir in sugar until well mixed.

Pack in small containers for one-meal servings.

To serve: Thaw at room temperature for 2 hours. Very good with pork, ham or poultry.

Storage time: 1 year.

BRANDY BUTTER

2 oz. butter   2 tbsp brandy
2 oz. icing sugar

Cream butter and sugar and work in brandy.

Pack in small waxed containers, pressing down well.

To serve: Thaw in refrigerator for 1 hour before serving with pudding or mince pies.

Storage time: 1 year.

BREAD SAUCE

1 small onion	2 oz. fresh white
4 cloves	breadcrumbs
½ pint milk	½ oz. butter
	Salt and pepper

Peel onion and stick with cloves. Put all ingredients into saucepan and simmer for 1 hour. Remove onion, beat sauce well, and season further to taste. Cool.

Pack in small waxed containers.

To serve: Thaw in top of double boiler, adding a little cream.

Storage time: 1 month.

CELERY AND HERB SCONES

8 oz. wholemeal	2 oz. butter
flour	1 level tsp basil
1 tsp baking powder	3 sticks celery
½ tsp bicarbonate of	5-oz. carton natural
soda	yogurt
½ tsp salt	

Sift together flour, baking powder, bicarbonate of soda and salt. Rub in butter until mixture is like fine breadcrumbs. Add basil and finely chopped celery and mix well. Using a knife, bind mixture with yogurt to form a soft dough. Pat out to a rectangle about ¾ in. thick on a floured board. Cut out into 1½ in.-diameter scones. Place on greased and floured baking tray and bake at 400°F (Gas Mark 6) for 12–15 minutes. Cool.

Pack in polythene bag.

To serve: Heat at 325°F (Gas Mark 3) for 20 minutes and serve hot with butter.

Storage time: 2 months.

BEER FRUIT LOAF

3 oz. butter
3 oz. soft brown
  sugar
3 oz. currants
1 oz. chopped mixed
  peel

8 oz. plain
  wholemeal flour
1 egg
¼ pint ale
½ tsp bicarbonate of
  soda

Cream the butter and sugar, and gradually work in fruit, peel and flour. Beat the egg with the ale, and stir in the bicarbonate of soda. Add to the butter and flour mixture, mix thoroughly and pour into 1-lb loaf tin which has been well greased. Bake at 350°F (Gas Mark 4) for 1 hour. Cool.

Pack in heavy-duty foil or polythene.

To serve: Thaw without wrappings at room temperature for 3 hours, and cut in slices to serve spread with butter.

Storage time: 4 months.

SIMPLE HONEY CAKE

4 oz. butter
2 oz. Barbados sugar
3 tbsp honey
2 lightly beaten eggs
8 oz. wholemeal
  flour

3 tsp baking powder
1 tsp ground
  cinnamon
Milk
1 oz. halved
  blanched almonds

Cream butter and sugar and work in honey. Add eggs, flour sifted with baking powder and cinnamon, and a little milk to make a smooth dropping consistency. Grease 7-in. square tin, and scatter almonds in the bottom. Pour in cake mixture and bake at 350°F (Gas Mark 4) for 1 hour. Cool.

Pack in heavy-duty foil or polythene.

To serve: Thaw without wrappings at room temperature for 3 hours.

Storage time: 4 months.

CHRISTMAS PUDDINGS

If there is no other storage space, rich fruit puddings can be made to traditional recipes, in foil bowls, covered with foil lids, and stored up to 1 year in the freezer.

MINCE PIES

Mince pies should not be stored longer than 1 month in the freezer, as mincemeat is highly spiced and may develop an 'off flavour' in the freezer. Pies may be baked and packed in cartons for freezing. If there is more space, pies may be frozen unbaked in their baking tins. Unbaked pies have better flavour and scent, and crisper and flakier pastry than pies baked before freezing.

DECEMBER

Short-storage items such as stuffings, party puddings and cakes, can be prepared and frozen at the beginning of the month. It is a good idea to make room for a few simple casseroles and puddings to use during the busy party days at the end of the month.

FOOD IN SEASON

Vegetables Brussels sprouts, cabbage, celery, Jerusalem artichokes, leeks, parsnips, swedes, turnips.
Fruit Apples, cranberries, grapes, pomegranates, tangerines.
Fish Cod, haddock, herring, mackerel, oysters, plaice, scallops, sole, sprats, turbot, whiting.
Meat, Poultry and Game Goose, turkey, hare, partridge, pheasant, snipe, wild duck.

WHAT TO BUY FROM THE SHOPS
Bread.

BULK BUYING CHECKLIST
Cream, ice cream, trifles, prepared party dishes, poultry, bacon, sausages, Brussels sprouts, peas, potato croquettes.

PREPARE-AHEAD DISHES

SAUSAGE STUFFING

1 lb sausage meat
2 oz. streaky bacon
Liver from turkey or
  chicken
1 onion
1 egg

2 oz. fresh white
  breadcrumbs
Salt and pepper
2 tsp fresh mixed
  herbs
Stock

Put sausage meat in a bowl. Mince bacon, liver and onion. Mix with sausage meat, egg, breadcrumbs, seasonings and herbs, and moisten with a little stock if necessary. Do not stuff bird in advance with sausage stuffing.

Pack in cartons or polythene bags.

To serve: Thaw in refrigerator for 12 hours before using to stuff bird.

Storage time: 2 weeks.

CHESTNUT STUFFING

1 lb chestnuts
2 oz. fresh white
  breadcrumbs
1 oz. melted butter

2 tsp fresh mixed
  herbs
2 eggs
Salt, pepper and dry
  mustard

Peel chestnuts, then simmer in a little milk until tender. Sieve and mix with breadcrumbs, butter, herbs and eggs. Add salt and pepper and a pinch of dry mustard.

Pack in cartons or polythene bags.

To serve: Thaw in refrigerator for 12 hours before stuffing the bird.

Storage time: 1 month.

POULTRY STUFFING

2 oz. suet	1 tsp chopped thyme
4 oz. fresh white breadcrumbs	Grated rind of ½ lemon
2 tsp chopped parsley	Salt and pepper
	1 medium egg

Mix all ingredients together, binding with egg. The stuffing may be frozen uncooked, or may be cooked as forcemeat balls. If a bird is to be stuffed for freezing, make sure both bird and stuffing are very cold, and that the bird remains cold during stuffing. The freezer life of a bird ready-stuffed will be only that of the stuffing (i.e. 1 month).

Pack stuffing into cartons or polythene bags. Deep-fried forcemeat balls may be packed in cartons or bags.

To serve: Thaw stuffing enough to use in poultry. Ready-cooked forcemeat balls can be put into a roasting tin with the poultry or into a casserole 10 minutes before serving time.

Storage time: 1 month.

TURKEY MOUSSE

12 oz. cold turkey	Salt and pepper
½ gill white sauce	1 gill whipped cream
¼ pint aspic jelly (made double strength)	

Mince turkey finely and pound it, gradually adding white sauce. If using commercial aspic, make up with half the given amount of water. Season well and fold in whipped cream. Set in a ring mould if possible, or otherwise in a soufflé dish which will go in the freezer.

Pack by covering mould or dish with lid of heavy-duty foil.

To serve: Thaw at room temperature for 2 hours, turn out and serve with a winter salad of watercress, chicory and green peppers. If a ring mould is used, the centre of the mousse can be filled with salad.

Storage time: 1 month.

TURKEY CAKES

1 lb cold turkey	½ gill gravy
Salt and pepper	1 tsp tomato purée
8 oz. cold potatoes	

Mince turkey, season and mix with mashed potato, gravy and tomato purée. Form into small flat cakes. Roll in crumbs or seasoned flour and fry on both sides until golden. Cool.

Pack in foil or polythene bag.

To serve: Reheat in oven or frying pan.

Storage time: 1 month.

CREAMED TURKEY

Cooked turkey	White sauce

Cut cooked turkey in neat pieces and bind with white sauce made with half turkey stock and half milk, and thickened with cornflour. Cool.

Pack in waxed containers.

To serve: Reheat in a double boiler, to use with toast or rice. A few mushrooms, peas or pieces of green pepper may be added. This may also be used as a filling for pies or flan cases.

Storage time: 1 month.

TURKEY ROLL

12 oz. cold turkey
8 oz. cooked ham
1 small onion
Pinch of mace
Salt and pepper

½ tsp mixed fresh
    herbs
1 large egg
Breadcrumbs

Mince turkey, ham and onion finely and mix with mace, salt and pepper and herbs. Bind with beaten egg. Put into greased dish or tin, cover and steam for 1 hour. This may be cooked in a loaf tin, a large cocoa tin lined with paper, or a stone marmalade jar. While warm, roll in breadcrumbs, then cool completely.

Pack in heavy-duty foil or in polythene bag.

To serve: Thaw at room temperature for 1 hour, and slice to serve with salads or sandwiches.

Storage time: 1 month.

CHOCOLATE PUDDING ICE

2 oz. halved stoned
    raisins
1½ oz. currants
½ oz. candied orange
    peel

1 oz. halved glacé
    cherries
Liqueur glass rum
    or brandy
1 pint chocolate ice
    cream

Soak raisins, currants, peel and cherries in rum or brandy overnight. Fold into slightly softened ice cream and pack into metal pudding mould. This may be used as a substitute for the traditional Christmas pudding for parties, and is good served with liqueur-flavoured cream.

Pack in metal pudding mould and cover with heavy-duty foil for storage. The ice may also be packed in waxed or rigid plastic containers.

To serve: Unmould and serve with cream if liked.

Storage time: 1 year.

CHOCOLATE LOG CAKE

3 oz. self-raising flour	2 drops vanilla essence
Pinch of salt	
1 oz. cocoa	*Icing:*
3 oz. butter or margarine	8 oz. icing sugar
	3 oz. butter
3 oz. caster sugar	2 oz. plain chocolate
2 eggs	1 tbsp hot water

Sieve flour, salt and cocoa. Cream fat and sugar until light and fluffy. Beat in eggs one at a time with a little of the flour mixture. Stir in remaining flour and essence. Spread evenly in a lined Swiss roll tin. Bake at 425°F (Gas Mark 7) for 10 minutes. Turn out on sugared greaseproof paper. Trim off edges and roll up quickly with paper inside. Make icing by shredding chocolate and melting in a basin with the hot water. Add to creamed butter and sugar and beat well. When cake is cold, unroll carefully and spread half the chocolate icing on the surface. Roll tightly and cover outside and ends with icing, decorating with a fork to resemble a log.

Pack by placing on oblong cake board and freezing before putting into polythene bag.

To serve: Remove from wrappings and thaw at room temperature for 3 hours. Dust with icing sugar and decorate with robin and holly.

Storage time: 2 months.

LIGHT CHRISTMAS CAKE

8 oz. butter
8 oz. caster sugar
4 large eggs
10 oz. plain flour
1 tsp baking powder
2 oz. chopped
  orange peel

3 oz. sultanas
3 oz. currants
2 oz. glacé cherries
3 oz. glacé pineapple
Grated rind of ½
  lemon
Milk

Cream butter and sugar until light and fluffy. Beat in eggs one at a time, adding a little flour each time. Gradually work in flour sifted with baking powder, and fruit (chop the cherries and pineapple), and grated lemon rind. Add a little milk if necessary to make a soft consistency. Grease and line 10-in. round tin and put in mixture. Bake at 350°F (Gas Mark 4) for 1½ hours. Cool.

Pack in heavy-duty foil or polythene.

To serve: Thaw at room temperature for 3 hours.

Storage time: 4 months.

CRANBERRY ORANGE CAKE

8 oz. plain flour
½ tsp salt
1½ tsp baking
  powder
½ tsp bicarbonate of
  soda
4 oz. cranberries

Grated rind and
  juice of 1 orange
8 oz. sugar
2 tbsp melted
  butter
1 egg
4 oz. chopped nuts

Sift together flour, salt, baking powder and bicarbonate of soda. Chop the cranberries. Grate the orange rind and add to the squeezed juice and butter and enough water to make 6 fl. oz. of liquid. Add the flour, sugar, egg, nuts and cranberries and beat well. Pour into buttered 1½-lb loaf tin and bake at 350°F (Gas Mark 4) for 1 hour. Cool in tin for 10 minutes, then on cake rack.

Pack in heavy-duty foil or polythene bag.

To serve: Thaw in wrappings at room temperature for 3 hours. Sprinkle with sifted icing sugar or ice with a light icing of orange juice and icing sugar.

Storage time: 4 months.

FÊTE GINGERBREAD

1 lb sweetened apple purée	½ oz. ground ginger
	½ oz. caraway seeds
8 oz. butter	2 fl. oz. brandy
1 lb plain flour	2 oz. candied peel

Prepare apple purée. Cream butter and work in purée, flour, ginger, caraway seeds and brandy. Cut peel in thin slices and add to mixture. Put into two greased and lined rectangular tins (about 8 by 12 in.) and bake at 350°F (Gas Mark 4) for 1 hour. Cool in tin.

Pack gingerbread in a slab in heavy-duty foil or polythene.

To serve: Thaw without wrappings at room temperature for 3 hours, and cut in small slices.

Storage time: 4 months.

INDEX